Praise for Geneen Roth

"Geneen Roth's early work pulled my sister out of the abyss of eating disorders. My gratitude and admiration for Geneen has deepened still with her newest book. In *This Messy Magnificent Life,* we experience her signature divine wisdom and hilarious humanity—but Geneen also gives us something new and important. Here, Geneen shows us how our individual body and food obsessions are directly linked to our collective oppression as women—and how getting free from our personal prisons is crucial to seeking liberation at every level. This is a beautiful, funny, deeply relevant book—a vital work for this moment."

—**Glennon Doyle**, author of the #1 *New York Times* bestseller *Love Warrior* and founder and president of Together Rising

"*This Messy Magnificent Life* delivers a brilliant, funny, and frank offering at the stroke of midnight (just when we need it). By page ten you're convinced she's your smartest and funniest best friend. *This Messy Magnificent Life* is—dare I say it? Yep. Messy. It's magnificent, hilarious, and 100 percent the generous, complicated gift that is Geneen Roth's imagination, experience, and soul, on a platter. 2018 will be made easier to navigate with *This Messy Magnificent Life* by my side."

—**Kathy Najimy**, actor, activist, director

"Geneen Roth's secret sauce—the ingredients of which are warmth, wisdom, honesty and powerful self-scrutiny—is all blended to perfection in this lovely book, which will be a welcome companion to her legions of readers, and bring her many lucky new ones. There's a reason she's such a treasure."

—**Dani Shapiro**, author of *Hourglass* and *Devotion*

"I've long admired Geneen Roth's approach to food and its place in our lives. In *This Messy Magnificent Life* she goes beyond food and shows the complex interconnection between our minds and the bodies we have the power to heal. Her insights and simple practices will help readers rediscover the power to live their most vibrant lives."

—**Mark Hyman, M.D.**, director of the Cleveland Clinic Center for Functional Medicine and #1 *New York Times* bestselling author of *Eat Fat, Get Thin*

"These chapters of simple advice are easily digestible, and reading one per day is a good way to start this practice. Empowering words for women—especially those struggling with body issues—to regain control of their lives."

—*Kirkus Reviews*

"Roth, who has become more resilient with age, will captivate readers with her energetic yet calming wisdom."

—*Publishers Weekly*

"Roth is an intellectual, but her tone is warm and comfortable, and she knows when to add a touch of humor. She willingly shares her own emotional baggage, and her advice is life-affirming."

—*Booklist*

"Now is the time to celebrate the qualities that make you unique and to be bold in your pursuit of personal bliss. This book will help get you started."

—*BookPage*

"Roth's pioneering work on mindful eating and spirituality has helped countless dieters do as the extreme yo-yo dieting author did herself: Make peace with food—or at least call a truce."

—NPR's *The Salt*

PREVIOUS BOOKS BY GENEEN ROTH

Lost and Found

Women Food and God

When Food Is Love

The Craggy Hole in My Heart and the Cat Who Fixed It

Breaking Free from Emotional Eating

Feeding the Hungry Heart

When You Eat at the Refrigerator, Pull Up a Chair

Appetites

Why Weight?

This Messy Magnificent Life

A Field Guide to Mind, Body, and Soul

GENEEN ROTH

SCRIBNER

New York   London   Toronto   Sydney   New Delhi

Scribner
An Imprint of Simon & Schuster, Inc.
1230 Avenue of the Americas
New York, NY 10020

The names and characteristics of some individuals in this book have been changed.

Illustrations by Kristen Haff, inspired by *From the Tide Pools to the Stars*
by Erin B. Hughes

First Scribner trade paperback edition January 2019

For information about special discounts for bulk purchases, please contact Simon
& Schuster Special Sales at 1-866-506-1949 or business@simonandschuster.com.

The Simon & Schuster Speakers Bureau can bring authors to your live event. For
more information or to book an event, contact the Simon & Schuster Speakers
Bureau at 1-866-248-3049 or visit our website at www.simonspeakers.com.

Interior design by Jill Putorti

Manufactured in the United States of America

10 9 8 7 6 5 4 3 2

Library of Congress Cataloging-in-Publication Data is available.

ISBN 978-1-5011-8246-4
ISBN 978-1-5011-8247-1 (pbk)
ISBN 978-1-5011-8248-8 (ebook)

For Max

Contents

Introduction by Anne Lamott   xi

Prologue: Dropping the Me Project   1

PART ONE:
AROUND THE TABLE

Chapter One: Manna   9

Chapter Two: The Last Bite   23

Chapter Three: Lasting Weight Loss   27

Chapter Four: Heavenly Bodies   35

Chapter Five: If I Were Gloria Steinem   43

Chapter Six: The Red String Project   51

Chapter Seven: In the End   63

PART TWO:
THROUGH THE MIND

Chapter Eight: Zen Mind, Puppy Mind   71

Chapter Nine: Be Kind to the Ghost Children   81

Chapter Ten: Hoodwinked by Suffering   97

Chapter Eleven: The Four-Month Virus   109

Chapter Twelve: Hummingbirds on My Fingers   119

Chapter Thirteen: Crushed Stars   129

Chapter Fourteen: What Remains   135

CONTENTS

PART THREE:
INTO THE SUBLIME

Chapter Fifteen: A Big Quiet   143

Chapter Sixteen: The Breaths I Have Left   153

Chapter Seventeen: Waiting for the Apocalypse   159

Chapter Eighteen: What Isn't Wrong   167

Chapter Nineteen: The Blue Vest   171

Chapter Twenty: Not Minding What Happens   181

Chapter Twenty-One: Snorkeling in the Night Sky   187

Epilogue: Stop Waiting to Be Ready   193

Last Words: Touchstones for Breaking the Trance   197

In Grateful Acknowledgment   201

Introduction by Anne Lamott

Just once, I'd like to read a piece on Geneen Roth that does not mention food.

All those thousands of articles over the years have driven home the radical message she carries, embodies, exudes—that food and weight are not the problem or the solution to the wound, or to the losses of so long ago that we try to numb or redeem by stuffing or starving or weighing or rejecting ourselves.

Yes, her pioneering books were among the first to link compulsive eating and perpetual dieting with deeply personal and spiritual issues that go far beyond food, weight, and body image. She changed my life twenty-five years ago when I read my first Geneen Roth book—the same day I swallowed ipecac in an effort to lose just five more pounds, which would make all of life spring into Technicolor, like when Dorothy lands in Oz. I had never before made the connection that the way we eat is the way we live—and that our relationship to food, our bodies, money, and love is an exact reflection of the amount of joy, presence, and oxygen we believe we are allowed to have in our lives.

Never before had someone expressed so brilliantly, and with such wit, that curiosity and self-love were the way home—not the latest diet, kale cleanse, or fair-trade coffee colonic.

So I discovered Geneen's writings on food, and was hooked. Yet there is just so much more to her.

For starters, there is the exuberantly real, and the cranky.

Geneen is brilliant about psychological and spiritual matters, the deepest levels of healing. She can speak with profound honesty before a thousand people who are moved to tears by her radical acceptance of who they are, and what they have thought and tried—sometimes for decades, often as recently as that morning. But she can also be a goofball with a wild imagination. Somehow she manages to be hilariously self-deprecating while also being militantly on her own side, moment by moment. She also invents new languages. Passages in this book made me laugh out loud.

There is her life with her pets, with whom she shares great comfort and joy, and gleans wisdom about restoring our primal connection to Love. I think she might have a pet disorder, though. You may have read her book about the sainted Blanche, her two-hundred-pound cat, or heard of her darling and elegant poodle Celeste. Or perhaps you've encountered Izzy, her current dog— who, ironically, has disturbing food issues, including anorexia. Izzy is the only dog I know that I can leave in my kitchen with the cat's bowl. (A portrait of Blanche, who was male, still hangs in a place of prominence in Geneen's living room, as might, in other homes, a painting of the Queen.)

There is her beloved Matt—her husband and best friend and foil, who conveniently shares the disorder regarding pets. I never think of one without the other. Astonishingly, Matt is very loving and gentle about her other fixation: fancy sweaters. As far as I know, he has never said a word when she has brought home the latest, although he does make a quiet keening noise. (None of us—including Geneen—knows what the sweater thing means, and I do not feel prepared to discuss it further here. I'm just saying.)

There is her smile, which is huge and irregular—one of a kind, almond-shaped, toothy, and frequent. She not only laughs at all my jokes, which I love in a girl, but laughs with infinite compassion at herself and her foibles, failures, victories, silliness, and ordinary human behavior.

There are her tears of empathy—for the child she was, for us all, for how hard it is here, for how deeply weird and impossible life and families can be, and for the world.

There is her contagious delight in the sensuous. I have seen her nibbling a bit of exquisite dark chocolate for whole minutes, as if it had to last her the month, savoring it as if God had given her and only her this one and only piece. Some of the essays in this book will help you learn to do this, too—while also teaching you radical forgiveness if you have recently set upon a sack of Halloween candy like a dog.

I love the depth of her spirituality, and her absolute, total commitment to it (along with the pets . . . and the chocolate . . . and the sweaters). I also love her plainsong erudition, which is in equal proportion to her thrilling humanity.

I can tell Geneen any horrible secret I may have, one that I believe reeks of depravity or madness or general loathsomeness, and she will hear me, and say the three greatest healing words on earth: "Oh, me too." She will reach out to stroke the back of my hand and smile that almond smile.

And man, can that girl pay attention. And so she knows. She knows our hearts, because she listens to hers. She pays attention to her best friends, to strangers, to God, to pets, to Matt, to her spiritual teachers, to the grasses and birds, to the cats, the dogs, the child.

Many pieces in this book, and in fact in Geneen's life's work, center on developing the trust and intimacy with one's own deepest self that are necessary for practicing radical self-care, awareness, and good boundaries. Perhaps as a result, Geneen is as generous as anyone I know. A few weeks ago we were on the phone and I mentioned that I was frantically cleaning my house because people were coming by for a fund-raiser for a village school I support in Myanmar. A few days later, her huge check arrived in the mail.

Geneen reads the same way she did as a little girl: as an act of devotion, discovery, salvation, meditation, and joy. This has helped her to hone her God-given gifts as a writer—her innate curiosity, her elegance and truth-telling, her brilliant or hilarious turns of phrase, her care.

Forgiveness is the center of her being, of her life. From that springs a deepening awareness of It All— one's tummy, the physical hunger; one's skin, longing for gentle touch and accepting eyes; one's body and its incarnational realms; one's heart, the umbilical link to

God; and what e.e. cummings called *the gay great happening illimitably earth.*

Oh, yes, the food stuff. Has anyone else's writings on compulsive eating and the healing of the heart, mind, and body thrown the lights on for more people, or changed the lives of more of us when we sit down to eat? Or pull up a chair at the fridge? Or open the half-pound bag of M&M's in the 7-Eleven parking lot? Has anyone else helped so many of us develop the muscles to keep ourselves company—loving company—when we're halfway through a sack of Cheetos, or starving ourselves yet again, or purging, or crying in a fluorescent-lit dressing room while trying on swimsuits?

Some of the stories in this book will give you insight and encourage self-forgiveness around money. And here is the scariest thing of all: this book will encourage you to become big and juicy and real, no matter what your parents, your teachers, and your culture have told you over the years.

There is a lot in this book about learning to make (or let) food be about food, and love be about love. There are also stories about the path of learning to trust yourself alone in a room with a cake—or, for that matter, a pile of bills, a clutch of memories, a family, or a set of deadlines. There are stories about true love, loneliness, and the places in between. There are stories about God, and writers, and parents, and gardens. But mostly these are stories about us, as told by Geneen.

*I'd tried versions of not
fixing myself before, but always
with the secret hope that not
fixing myself would fix me.*

Dropping the Me Project

From the beginning, I was always more anxious than the average bear. I was told at various times that I was too sensitive, too emotional (i.e., too female), too big, too curious, too demanding, too intense. The adults somehow forgot to mention that I was also sassy, silly, and keen-eyed. Regrettably, gaining and losing the same fifteen pounds every few weeks did not improve my self-worth. So at age twenty-four, I started looking for a way to handle "the full catastrophe," as Zorba the Greek described living.

At the start—during the 1980s—my focus was on untangling misguided beliefs about food. Along with most women who struggled with their weight, I believed that if I could resolve what seemed to be the source of my self-hatred, I would be thin, happy, free. It made so much sense: take away the source of the pain and the pain will go away, leaving a bright spirit in its place.

As I lost weight, I quickly understood that issues with food were cover-ups. Yes, they needed to be addressed on the physical level, otherwise they could turn into more serious illnesses. And yes, most of us needed to learn what our bodies longed for and needed, because we'd been brainwashed into craving junk, but the genesis of compulsive eating was not physical, and unless its source was addressed, a range of equally painful behaviors would emerge.

When my misery with food ended—and didn't change anything except the size of my thighs—I kept trying to fix other broken parts of myself by immersing myself in therapy, intensive meditation retreats, and rigorous spiritual practices. Now, I think of these last thirty years as similar to the wandering period in the Buddha's life, minus a few essentials like his willingness to sleep on nails and eat one measly grain of rice a day. Furthermore, it took him twenty-nine years less than me to catch on to the truth. In my own case, it was only recently that I was willing to relinquish the Me Project and stop trying to fix what had never been broken. I'd tried versions of not fixing myself before, but always with the secret hope that not fixing myself would fix me. This time I only wanted one thing: to be at home in my mind and life as I knew it.

I used the same practices I'd used to end my suffering with food. If being vigilant about stopping the harshness with which I treated myself had unraveled the most obsessive behavior pattern of my life, if allowing my full range of feelings without acting on them had dismantled my suffering with food, why wouldn't it dismantle what caused it: the ongoing, low-level discontent of what it felt like to be me? And finally, if being resolute about feeding myself with awareness and a large dose of kindness changed how I ate, why wouldn't it change how I lived? What if, as I once did and still do with food, I could live as if nothing was broken, nothing was wrong, while nonetheless questioning the constellation of beliefs that led to anxiety, isolation, and self-hatred? What if I believed what Zen teacher Shunryu Suzuki said: that we are all perfect and that we need some improvement? Or, as they say in Texas, God loves you exactly the way you are; and she loves you too much to let you stay like this.

*   *   *

Freedom from mental suffering is not a mystery, but a willingness to examine what keeps us from directly experiencing the deep-blue peace and quiet joy that are always accessible and forever unaffected by the passing show.

This Messy Magnificent Life is about the path I followed and the obstacles I encountered along the way. It also challenges the conviction that everyday ease and freedom, no matter what the external situation, are reserved for the very few—that is, not for poor doomed Little Match Girl *moi*.

The book starts where *Women Food and God* ended: around the table, because the way we eat is always a primary gateway to the mind that creates the suffering about it. My ongoing work with retreat students—their stories and their breathtaking changes—continues to provide a groundwork for not only the work with food but also with an assortment of everyday doorways like illness, anxiety, hatred, misogyny, intimate relationships, and the guy paying with change in the express line.

This Messy Magnificent Life chronicles the shift from feeling as if we are secretly defective, helpless, and too often walking on the barbed wire of our thoughts, to waking up with the ever-present, always-sublime freedom from our incessantly restless minds, right in the middle of ordinary life.

Freedom from mental suffering is not a mystery, but a willingness to examine what keeps us from directly experiencing the deep-blue peace and quiet joy that are always accessible and forever unaffected by the passing show. If the drama and chaos in the outside world are expressions of the minds that create them, then naming and questioning the way we live in these minds, and on this earth, is the only way that true change can happen.

And so, we begin.

PART ONE

Around
the Table

Attention is everything. Without it, all else is a temporary fix and no long-lasting change is possible.

CHAPTER ONE

Manna

I am making a cup of tea in my favorite purple-flowered mug when I smell smoke. I look through the windows behind me and see plumes of smoke through the trees. I call the fire department and they tell me there is a fire down the road, that it's not contained, and that we might have to evacuate our home. They'll let me know. My husband, Matt, is away—he never seems to be around during the panoply of biblical California disasters (earthquakes, fires, mudslides)—so I will have

9

to deal with this myself. My heart races. I feel panicked. But then I think, "This will be fine. Sometimes bad is good." I remember a haiku by Zen teacher Masahide that I read just yesterday: Barn's burnt down, now I can see the moon.

Since I have the luxury of time, I walk around the house looking at the things we've accumulated—my mother's antique Bombay chest, doors from Bali, a cabinet from Japan. The photographs of Matt and me at our wedding, of my mother and me at my twin nephews' bar mitzvahs last year. I put five framed pictures and three photo albums in a pile near the front door.

I walk into my closet and I look around, a bit dazed. All these clothes. The only time my father hinted that he knew he was dying was a few weeks after he was diagnosed with stage-four lymphoma, when we were walking past his closet. He said, "My clothes. What's going to happen to all my clothes?" As if they had lives of their own and would miss his legs, his arms, his wrists, or had meaning beyond his insatiable hunger for things and his inability to understand the meaning of enough.

I look blankly at my shoes, my sweaters, my pants. If our house burns down and I am left with only the clothing I take now, what would I want? What can't I live without? I finger an embroidered jacket, think about throwing it in my car, but then I realize I haven't worn it in a year and although it was once my favorite piece of clothing, it isn't now. I leave it hanging next to the black wool jacket with the short sleeves and the distressed gray corduroy jacket.

I call my neighbor Susan—whose husband is a volunteer firefighter—to find out if she knows anything more about the fire. "What fire?" she asks, voice rising. And then Susan begins to scream. "I'm in a wheelchair! I'm alone! I've just had back surgery! I can't move!" I find myself thinking of the movie *Sorry, Wrong Number*, when the wheelchair-bound Barbara Stanwyck overhears a plan to commit a murder that turns out to be her own, but I keep this thought to myself. I tell Susan I will pick her up if we need to evacuate.

I move slowly, as if underwater. I put jewelry in a backpack—my wedding ring, my father's Masonic ring that he wore until the day he died, my grandmother's earrings, my mother's enameled snake bracelet, my father's first watch. I zip up the backpack, walk out to the car, and put the bag in the trunk. I can't decide if I am numb or if I am enlightened because I've taken nothing else besides my purse, a computer, the stuffed toy pencil my first editor left me when she died, medicine, some underwear, the photograph albums, my favorite sweatshirt, our house insurance policy, our dog.

I call the sheriff's office. They tell me they are going door-to-door and asking people to evacuate; it is not yet mandatory for our particular road, but soon may be. I decide to preempt the evacuation order, take the dog, call and pick up Susan, and leave, grateful that the flames I saw haven't cut off my escape down our one-lane road. At least I am alive. I dial Matt's number from the car and remember the call I placed to him on a Russian icebreaker in Antarctica a few years ago. (Hi honey, no one died, but Bernie Madoff's been arrested and we've lost every cent of our money.)

As I drive I keep thinking about my jackets, my father, our stuff. About what enough actually is. Then, for some reason, I remember my college friend Linda. It was my senior year and I was a dinner guest at Linda's mother's house. Linda and I were bingeing buddies. She was the one who shared a gallon of Breyer's vanilla fudge twirl ice cream with me, and mined for the chocolate veins with her fingers. The one who, when making a batch of Toll House chocolate chip cookies, used the entire recipe to bake two huge cookies. That way, she told me, we only eat one cookie apiece.

At her mother's house, Linda was sitting at the head

of the table, scooping out ice cream into delicate porcelain bowls with violets and geraniums painted on their lips. Each one was passed around the table until everyone but me had their dessert. I looked at Linda and said, "This one's for me." She nodded her head. "I get it," she said, and proceeded to pile so much ice cream in the bowl that it began to drip down the red dahlias painted on the side of the bowl. The fact that I was already full from the dinner of fried oysters and gumbo didn't factor into my desire for that ice cream, not for one second.

My motto was that if some was good, more had to be better. I was haunted by a wild hunger for something I couldn't name, and while food didn't fill it, having more of what I didn't want was better than having nothing at all.

The word *manna* comes from the Hebrew word *mah*, which means "what," or "what is it?" In Exodus the Torah says, ". . . in the morning there was a fall of dew about the camp. When the fall of dew lifted, there, over the surface of the wilderness, lay a fine and flaky substance, as fine as frost on the ground. When the Israelites saw it, they said to one another, 'What is it?'—for they did not know what it was" (16:13–15). And, a few verses later, ". . . and so the House of Israel named it manna" (16:31). Each day, when they awoke and greeted the day, they would say "What is it?" for every day this manna was new, fresh, different from the day before. And no matter how much manna each person gathered, it was always exactly what that person needed—and although it tasted different to each person, it left each one satisfied and nourished. They couldn't store manna, hang it in their closets, or put it in the refrigerator like leftover pizza. They couldn't buy it, barter it, or use it against each other; there was only enough manna for that day. And no one had more than anyone else. But somehow, manna miraculously appeared each morning for forty years of wandering in the desert.

Man, oh man. From that perspective, refrigeration and closets sure messed things up. Because now we are wandering in the desert again, but this time, it's the wilderness of too much. Of feeling perpetually discontent and hungry for more, even when our bellies and our houses are stuffed.

Halfway into an eating meditation at a retreat, a time when most people are no longer hungry, I ask people to put down their forks, take a breath, and stop eating. "Jesus," I hear someone mutter, "just when I was getting going."

I look around the room. Donna's fork is in the air, ready for the next bite. Her mouth is still filled with food. After she swallows the current bite, she says, "I am hesitant to mention this but I am really full—like a twelve on a scale of one to ten. But I don't want to stop. Period. And you can't make me."

I tell Donna she's right. I can't make her stop. And in any case, force, cajoling, and exerting willpower have all proved incredibly ineffective where compulsive eating is concerned. But, I tell her, I am nonetheless curious about two things: who she is taking me to be at the moment, and what she hopes that continuing to eat will give her.

"My mother," she answers, almost before I finish speaking. "You are definitely my mother. She put me on a diet when I was two, and I've been on one ever since. And the answer to your second question is more. Just more. If I put the fork down, if I stop eating, I feel deprived. I'm not sure if I'm feeling sad or lost or empty when the food is all gone, but I'm sure I want more."

———— ✑ ————

We don't know what we're feeding, but we know we want more. We're not sure what the sadness is about or why we feel inconsolable, but we're sure the solution is to take more, have more, eat more. As if the answer to everything that makes us uncomfortable is more. As if it's a choice between having more of what we don't want or nothing at all.

A beloved spiritual teacher once told me that I kept protecting myself from losses that had already happened. I kept dragging the past into the present, and carried it into the future. The deprivation of childhood, the scarcity of tenderness and of belonging—and my attempts to rectify them—kept repeating themselves because that's all I knew. I had no language for sufficiency, no way to see it, no way to recognize what was actually in front of me. "If a pickpocket had stood before Jesus," another teacher said, "all he would see is pockets." We see what we believe. When we look at the world with hungry eyes, we only see lack; everything—people, meals, situations—looks like food we are desperate for. But the second we name what we are doing, the second we pay attention to it, we are no longer merged with it. We are no longer wandering in the desert or hoarding bowls of ice cream or starving for love. We are the awareness that notices that we are wandering in the desert, hoarding ice cream, starving for love. Attention is everything. Without it, all else is a temporary fix and no long-lasting change is possible.

Most of us already know this; we've tried hundreds of quick fixes: diets, affirmations, workshops that promise abundance, instant changes. Sometimes I ask a group of people how many of them have been on a diet. They all raise their hands. Then I ask how many people lost weight on that diet. All hands are raised again. Then: How many people gained weight on said diet? Again, everyone. Finally, the last question: How many people believe that another diet is the answer now? Everyone. We don't want to know what we already know.

This is the part about having enough that has nothing to do with food. And this is the harder part because we live in a culture that worships more. We are so brainwashed into believing that more is better that we no longer question what it costs or whether it adds anything to our lives. We keep believing that there is an elusive tipping point when more will finally become enough, but no matter how thin we get or how much money we make, that point doesn't get any closer. And in the meantime we spend our days riding the roller coaster of dissatisfaction, discontent, and disease. (Or, as one of my students said, "I would die to be as thin as I was five years ago, when I would have died to have been thinner.") Until a disaster comes along, like being given a terminal diagnosis or evacuating your house because there's a fire down the road. Then, suddenly, the urgency of what is happening breaks the trance of more. And after the panic subsides, we find ourselves right smack in the middle of the fragile, unrepeatable, never-ending now—which, it turns out, is the only place from which we can ever know what enough is.

When my husband, Matt, and I lost almost every cent of our money in 2008, I was terrified, then I was ashamed, and then I panicked. As I wrote in *Lost and Found*, upon hearing my financial news, my teacher Jeanne said that "nothing of value was lost." To which I replied, "Now is not the time to be spiritual." But I soon realized that just as I'd had a choice with food (to suffer or not), I had a choice at that moment as well. I could keep panicking and focus on the fact that Matt and I had just lost thirty years of life savings and didn't have enough money to get through the next month, or I could realize, as the Zen teacher John Tarrant puts it, that "the sun still shines and you can still drink your coffee and the birds still call in the morning . . . and you can find out that what you came to this planet for is not necessarily your apartment."

In the end, I did both. But each time I descended into the hell realms of shame, I knew I would feel worse. And each time I made a choice to bring my attention back to the fact that I could still breathe, walk, and drink tea from my favorite purple mug, I felt lighter and happier than I'd been in a long time, even before we'd lost all our money.

That seemed magical to me. But then I realized that before we lost our money I was entranced by lack and the worry of not enough. And after losing our money I kept choosing to focus on this breath, this step, because when I listened to my thoughts—and focused on all we'd lost, and on what we were going to do, and how dumb we'd been to put all our money in one place—I felt as if I was going insane. The difference wasn't the money, since I'd felt we didn't have enough when we did, and that we did have enough when we'd lost everything. The difference was where I chose to place my attention, and that I became fierce about not descending into the nightmare of my thoughts. Having enough came down to moment-to-moment choices of attention.

———— ✍ ————

A woman once asked a spiritual teacher why she could remain so uninterested in her thoughts (and, therefore, remain present) during a retreat, but when she got home and started washing the dishes, her mind wandered into the past and future. He responded that "At a retreat you think what you're doing is important. But once you get home, you forget what you love more than your thoughts."

* * *

It's as if we slide back and forth between the desire for more (love, earrings, experiences) and fear that we will lose what we already have.

In biblical moments—when there's a threat of a fire, or you lose your money, or you get a life-threatening diagnosis—the urgency forces you back into the present moment and you suddenly realize how much you've been missing. You see the extraordinary in the ordinary. You pay attention to what has been here all along. The purple teacup. The trill of the whip-poor-will outside your window. The sensation of your feet touching the floor in the middle of the night. You look, as the poet

Mary Oliver says, "on the deeper level, from the heavenly visibles to the heavenly invisibles."

Later in the afternoon on the day that Susan and I evacuated our homes, we were notified that the fire was contained. After helping her back into her house, I walked (back) into mine with the dog, photograph albums, sweatshirt, computer, and jewelry. The awe at having a home and for all the things—heat, roof, walls, showers, refrigerators, food—I take for granted burned through my usual trance of managing "one damn thing after another" (as Churchill described history). For that evening and the many weeks that followed, I was awash in thank you, thank you, thank you. For being alive, for being given another day with a roof over my head. For having love, sky, breath.

My teacher Jeanne once said, "You do very well in catastrophes, Geneen. You notice what's important. The fact that you are alive, breathing, sensing, taking in what's around you, becomes primary. But the challenge is doing that on any old day, every day. You have to want this more than you want anything. You have to keep paying attention to the effulgence of every day."

It's as if we slide back and forth between the desire for more (love, earrings, experiences) and fear that we will lose what we already have. In the movement from one pole to the other, we are always whirling in the trance of deficiency in which we equate being alone with loneliness, restraint with deprivation, being silent with being empty. Or at least I do. I get seduced by the promise of adding yet another ornament to the tree of myself and forget to pay attention to the heavenly invisibles. And then I remember. And then I forget. And remember again.

Every meal disappears,
every vacation ends, dogs and cats
(not to mention a raft of people we love)
die before we do, and we are old ten
minutes after we are rosy-cheeked,
dewy-faced children. Bummer.

CHAPTER TWO

The Last Bite

I am sitting at the kitchen table enraptured with a bowl of tomato soup. Not just any tomato soup: mine has crushed tomatoes, coconut milk, sea salt, parsley, a dash of coconut oil, and honey. (If you try it at home, blend to a thick consistency, add some thyme, pepper, and cloves.) I look down at the bowl: a nip, not even a spoonful, is left. Although I'm no longer hungry, I still want more. Not of the tomato soup but of rapture. I am like my retreat student Uma, who said, "I feel bereft

23

when I'm full because I can't think of one thing, not one, that is better than what's in my mouth. And so I keep eating to avoid the ending of goodness."

And therein lies the problem, not just with food but with all things temporal. Every meal disappears, every vacation ends, dogs and cats (not to mention a raft of people we love) die before we do, and we are old ten minutes after we are rosy-cheeked, dewy-faced children. Bummer.

*　　*　　*

Bingeing—consistently eating beyond enough—is a way to not have to face that what we love ends.

I look back down at my might-as-well-be-empty bowl; I think again of my students and their reluctance, which is now my reluctance, to stop eating. Putting the spoon down feels like falling into the crack between worlds, like the ending of every relationship I didn't want to end, like being cut loose from the mother ship.

I went to a friend's memorial service the other day. When his wife of forty-two years spoke, she said, "He was here and now he's not. I just can't believe a person could disappear like this." Later she told me that she'd gained ten pounds since he died. "Chocolate ice cream helps," she said. "Eating gives me something to do. And it gives me something to feel besides grief. I walk around feeling very full. Empty but also full."

As I listened to her, I realized that every time we stop eating when our bodies have had enough, we face a little death. We face emptiness, zip, even for a second. Which is of course why people find bingeing (i.e., not stopping) so helpful, albeit excruciating. Bingeing—consistently eating beyond enough—is a way to not have to face that what we love ends.

Today, at least, I put the spoon down and decide not to take a second helping. I sit at the table listening to the silence, the space between eating and not eating. Between one breath and another. And in the quiet, which is another name for emptiness, I hear the sound of the wind in the live oak trees. I look up from the table and see the sun illuminating a square patch of kitchen floor. The background birdsong suddenly becomes foreground, and I realize once again that jewels are scattered everywhere, not just at the table. And only when I stop eating do I hear or see or know them.

> *When we don't believe or
> understand that weight serves
> a crucial purpose, we feel as if having a
> thin body is like being shot into the
> open sky without a space suit.*

CHAPTER THREE

Lasting Weight Loss

Two women I know have each had two lap band/ gastric sleeve procedures. Not one, but two operations in which they volunteered to have their bodies cut open and risk dying from surgical mistakes. All four of the operations did exactly what they were supposed to do, and the women did indeed lose weight. But each time they discovered creative ways to commit sabotage. They ate small amounts, all day long. They ate until they felt as if they would burst. And six months later the weight started coming back.

The million-dollar answer to the question of why weight loss is so difficult to maintain, is that along with the exaltation of being thin come less positive feelings. The lightness that accompanies an unencumbered body feels vulnerable. And if we've used our weight in any way, even unconsciously, to keep us safe, the joy of weight loss can be overlaid by a wash of terror. In my experience, one of the unspoken reasons why many people don't maintain their weight loss is that they don't want to be thinner more than they want to stay protected. Or hidden.

In my twenties, a few days from attempting suicide, I realized that I'd been speaking to myself in a language—eating uncontrollably—that I hadn't bothered to learn or understand. I decided—and this was the most radical and decidedly counterintuitive part—that I would trust the longing at the root of the compulsion rather than believing I was a self-destructive maniac. And once I took that leap and began trusting myself with food—my friends looked at me in horror when I ate whatever I wanted those first few weeks—everything changed.

The ongoing question was no longer what I could do to control my insanity, but what the eating could teach me. I saw almost immediately that every time I lost weight, I flung myself at unavailable men and then got consumed by the drama of convincing someone who didn't and would never want me to want me— which, being an impossible task, took up quite a lot of time.

I felt so unattractive at eighty pounds over my natural weight that flinging my body hither and thither was out of the question. And so I joined a writing class and started to write daily—something I'd longed to do since fifth grade—and quickly understood that if I got involved with yet another unavailable man, my creativity would focus on inventing interesting ways to capture he-who-had-no-interest-in-me. I decided to pour that creative energy into writing (instead). When I figured out that I could do for myself what eating had been unconsciously doing, I realized I'd been attempting to get through to myself with food, and vanilla fudge ice cream lost its allure. Even when I gained weight those first few weeks (because I didn't quite believe I wasn't going to punish myself with food again, so I figured I might as well eat as much as I could before the ax fell), I never went back to dieting or believing I was out of control.

When we don't believe or understand that weight serves a crucial purpose, we feel as if having a thin body is like being shot into the open sky without a space suit. We are supposed to know how to breathe without a mask, move in a body that is no longer weighted down, relate to people without layers of padding. And we are supposed to feel thrilled about the whole process even when the pounds we shed served us in oh-so-many ways.

* * *

Instead of avoiding fear we can do what is counterintuitive: welcome it and notice that the part that allows the fear is much bigger than the fear itself.

If you ask a group of people who want to lose weight whether they'd find being thinner threatening, you would hear a unanimous *No*. But you would be asking adults, and that which wants to stay hidden is young. The proof is not in what people say they want, but in what they do. Not in their wishes, but in their actions, which consistently lead to the spectacularly dismal results of maintaining weight loss. And while it is the adult who decides to limit her food or eat the Paleo diet or substitute good fats for trans fats, it is the ghost children—the ones that hid in the closet when our parents were fighting, or whose breasts our uncles fondled, or whose mother died when we were ten—who sabotage the results. If even just a part of us is constellated around a painful story from the past, if we haven't named or allowed the feelings that accompany that story their due, then losing weight is like telling a small child that everything on which her survival depends has been ripped away. Not exactly a recipe for success.

The heart of any addiction—drugs, alcohol, sex, money, food—is the avoidance of pain coupled with the unwillingness to acknowledge that both the behavior and its consequences serve us even as they destroy our lives. They keep us distracted from the original pain by creating another, possibly life-threatening situation. When we have to focus our attention on not driving while drunk, or having an operation to limit the food we eat so that we can walk, we have little time or interest in naming and meeting feelings we've been exiling for thirty or forty years.

Losing weight may indeed bring up fear of being overwhelmed by the very feelings you've used food to exile. But so what? Fear isn't a monster; it's a feeling. And like any feeling, it passes. Fear can be felt, held, dissolved by naming it, feeling its location in our bodies. Instead of avoiding fear we can do what is counterintuitive: welcome it and notice that the part that allows the fear is much bigger than the fear itself.

*   *   *

If we deprive and shame ourselves with food (or any other area of our lives), we will be deprived, ashamed beings who might also be thin for five minutes.

Maintaining weight loss isn't about what we eat, not really. It comes back to what we want from our brief time here on earth. It's about making a commitment to act in ways that match that desire, including our relationships to people, the work we do, the food we eat—and not giving ourselves the wiggle room of thinking we can go on a diet to lose weight and *then* pay attention to what drives us to food. Alas, it doesn't work like that. How we get there is who we will be when we arrive there. If we deprive and shame ourselves with food (or any other area of our lives), we will be deprived, ashamed beings who might also be thin for five minutes.

"Make no mistake about people who leap from burning windows," David Foster Wallace wrote. "Their terror of falling from a great height is still just as great as it would be for you or me. . . . The variable here is the other terror, the fire's flames: when the flames get close enough, falling to death becomes the slightly less ter-rible of two terrors."

Choosing to keep struggling with food, whether it's our way up or down the scale, is a choice to stay in the burning building of suffering while telling ourselves we can't help it. The other choice is to jump from the burning building and discover, according to Chögyam Trungpa, that "you're falling through the air, nothing to hang on to, no parachute. The good news is there's no ground."

> *I thought of my body as a
> collection of limbs and organs that
> happened to be connected to the person
> I took myself to be. It was like owning
> a three-story house and living in
> the attic for sixty-four years.*

CHAPTER FOUR

Heavenly Bodies

After breaking my back in an accident several years ago, it occurred to me that I hadn't realized I had a back. Not really. Yes, I knew the word for back. I knew my back was behind my front. I knew what a vertebra was from photos in freshman biology. I knew that when I did Pilates twice a week, it sometimes hurt back there. But as a longtime runner, dancer, and mountainhiker, I'd always treated my body like a machine I could push to its limits, like a piece of clay I could sculpt to my image of it. I thought of my body as a collection of limbs and organs that happened to be connected to the person I took myself to be. It was like owning a three-story house and living in the attic for sixty-four years.

In her book *M Train*, Patti Smith asks, "How is it that we never completely comprehend our love for someone until they're gone?" A version of the same question might be asked for backs that support us, legs that carry us, arms that pick up our children, and even for having bodies at all. In my own case, it took breaking my back to recognize the good fortune of having one.

Until the broken vertebrae (and the radical pain that ensued), I was both mystified and bored by what I'd heard other people call "living in the body." It felt uninteresting and irrelevant. It also felt unnecessary since everything I wanted to do—move, work, touch, eat, sleep, talk—could and did happen without occupying the lower floors. As usual, it took a crisis to wake me up; this time, to the difference between having a body and living in it.

The vertebral mishap made it clear that I'd been treating my body with unconscious resentment. "Really?" I'd think. "I have to interrupt what I am doing and work out with weights three times weekly to keep my bones strong? I have to stand up every twenty minutes when

I am writing because 'sitting is the new smoking'? And I have to practice Kegel exercises called Closing the Garage Door and Snapping the Turtle Shut so that I don't end up wearing Depends?"

It didn't stop there. There was also the day-to-day maintenance of flossing, water-picking, deep skin cleansing, and food preparation, just to wake up the next morning and do it over again. To that full-time job, add the hours of reading about and ordering the array of sunscreens that don't give you cancer, hair thickeners that don't make you look as if you stuck your finger in an electric socket, and toe-separators for bunions.

When I bring up the subject of embodiment at my retreats, the response is equally unenthusiastic. "For God's sake," my students say, "now I have to pay attention to MY BODY? My children need to be picked up from school. I have a business to run, a paper to write. Can't you just tell me what, when, and how much to eat? (So that I can do it for a few weeks and then rebel against being told what, when, and how much to eat?) No one ever told me that living in my body was part of the deal here. And I don't have time to learn something new." Yes, I say, I understand, after which I often quote James Joyce: "Mister Duffy lived a short distance from his body." A wave of head-nodding ensues, after which someone murmurs, "But the real problem is that my mother made me go on a diet when I was ten," and we are back in the attic again watching childhood reruns.

In the movie *The Story of Stuff*, the narrator says there is no such thing as "away" when we throw something away. It's all connected: the plastic bag in your hand, the shirt you just bought, the poisoning of the oceans. "There is no away," I kept saying to myself in those first post-fracture months, because although I did not believe that I was to blame for breaking my back, I did see that for many years I'd treated my body as a dumpster into which I could throw any food my mind wanted without consequences, as if the sheer physicality of this body and the intangibility of my mind (aka the real me) were unrelated.

*   *   *

When we actively notice and occupy
the body we already have, we begin noticing
. . . that blazing, animating life force
that allows the rest to be visible.

I was kinder to my jade plant than to my body.

I treated my cell phone with more reverence than I treated my body.

And yet.

While living in our bodies rather than a short distance from them would help us be alert and awake in our daily lives, it is also true that, despite the wishes of Walt Disney, who lies frozen in a crypt waiting to be sprung back to life when we discover the secret to immortality, bodies are not meant to last forever. Even if we spend ninety years treating these bodies magnificently, they will wear out and die. Or they will be hit by a truck, a stray bullet, or a renegade virus and die young. There is also the possibility that, like an increasing number of tourists, we will die by selfie while standing, say, on the top of Machu Picchu and falling to the bottom.

And there it is: the D word. "Life is like stepping onto a boat which is about to sail out to sea and sink," writes Zen teacher Shunryu Suzuki.

It's impossible to talk about bodies without also talking about death because whether we work out frantically or vacate the floors below the attic, bodies die. But as temporary, fragile, and vulnerable as our bodies are, they are the most direct portals to the only forever there is.

In the last few weeks of my father's life, days were measured in breaths, not minutes. Even the division of mornings sliding into afternoons rolling into evenings disappeared. Only this sip of water, these moistened lips, this exact moment mattered. Since I'd been four years old, I'd dreaded the death of my father, convinced that when he died I would die. But now I attended to only this breath, this sip of water.

Although I had an extraordinary and complicated relationship with my father, I was closer to him when he was dying than when he was healthy. And it wasn't because he couldn't talk back to me (well, maybe just a little), or comment on the Bach sonatas I played at his bedside. It was because death loomed so large that my mind could do nothing but give up its relentless drone and notice that nothing was missing, nothing was wrong. Every ragged breath was complete. Every time I dropped the cloth in the water, lifted it to his mouth, touched his lips—eons converged, melted, expanded. Universes were born, died, and were born again in the time it took to change his T-shirt. Every now was an eternity. (If I'd been a more skillful meditator, I would have probably discovered the same thing when sitting on a cushion, but I'm not, and I didn't.)

After he took his last breath, I closed my father's eyes, held his hand, and watched his face. During the next few hours, I kept looking for him in what remained—his familiar smell, baby-smooth hands, knobby nose—but he was gone. I don't know where he went, but it was as if he'd dropped his body like one of his Gucci loafers. Since his arms and legs were there but he wasn't, I had the thought that as the Indian sage Nisargadatta says, "we are not in our bodies—our bodies are in us."

Besides sitting with a dying person, the best way I know to be in daily contact with what never dies is to be awake now. To use the senses as a portal to what lies beyond them. Because the body's sensations are immediate, noticing them cuts through the babble of the mind that is always lurching from the past to the future, nattering on about details, hopes, and desires. On the horizontal level of day-to-day maintenance, digital devices, Kegel exercises, and toe-separators keep this so-called life going, but they are not life itself, just as clouds are not the sky.

St. Francis of Assisi said, "What we are looking for is what is looking." When we only pay attention to the ever-changing parade of thoughts, we miss what is looking. But when we actively notice and occupy the body we already have, we begin noticing what Eckhart Tolle calls the inner body. That blazing, animating life force that allows the rest to be visible. The part of us that has never, not for a second, gone away, and that eventually drops this body like a tight shoe.

*　　*　　*

You didn't float to your desk, you
didn't get beamed from your bedroom to
your kitchen. . . . Did you see what you
were looking at? . . . Or are you rummaging
around in the attic of your mind?

Here's my suggestion. Spend five minutes a day (every-one has five minutes), in segments of a minute apiece, noticing where you are. Just that much. You didn't float to your desk, you didn't get beamed from your bedroom to your kitchen. Your foot touches the floor, step-step-step on your way, you pass other objects, you hear a panoply of hums, noises, clatter. Did you see what you were look-ing at? Listen to what you were hearing? Are you here? Or are you rummaging around in the attic of your mind?

A breath, when you are noticing it, takes eons to fill your chest and leave it. When you become aware of the sound of the wind, the blare of a horn, the click of a computer key, you can't help being aware of the life force that expresses itself through this fragile body. And while immortality is not an option (I'm talking to you, Walt), when you fully drop into what you see or feel in your body, time falls away because it has no relevance. You cannot help but open to what gives it radiance: eternity itself—4.6 billion years of stardust. And we have it because we are it.

*Expecting a woman to
stand up for what she knows
while convincing her that she must
first be thin is like binding a Chinese
woman's feet and asking her
to run a marathon.*

CHAPTER FIVE

If I Were Gloria Steinem

My friend Dave (quoting from multiple sources) once told me that "A friend is someone you call when you need to move. A good friend is someone you call when you need to move a body." Isabel is the body-moving kind of friend. Recently, though, she has become a conspiracy theorist. She is convinced that there is a Cabal, a congregation of evil lizard-people called the Draco, whose intent is to control and ultimately destroy humanity. According to her, the attacks of September 11 were orchestrated by the Cabal; so were the Paris attacks, and ISIS itself. Also *Vanity Fair*, *Vogue*, most movie stars, politicians, and all billionaires are part of, or controlled by, the Cabal. (Isabel maintains that for selling your soul the Cabal grants you fame, success, and gushes of money, after which you are forever owned by them.) She says, "It's like *The Matrix*, but in real life. We are puppets of the Cabal. We think we are free, but we're being hypnotized and manipulated by the ones in power."

"How do I know I'm not part of the Cabal?" I ask her. "Maybe they got to me in my sleep."

"You're not important enough," she says.

But despite all the websites Isabel cites, the so-called evidence she reels off, I don't believe in the Cabal or in objective evil. I do believe there are, and have always been, confused, misguided people who commit insane acts. Although it seems as if there is an insane world "out there," it makes no sense to me that there is an out there that isn't also in here; in different circumstances—with no money, no food, and the promise of a heavenly afterlife—I, too, would be capable of violence.

It already doesn't take much for well-fed, velvet-clothed me to believe that those who cross me (the aggressive driver on the freeway, the basketball analyst

Charles Barkley when he disses Steph Curry, anyone who disagrees with me) are my enemies and must be vanquished.

The day after my conversation with Isabel, I heard Gloria Steinem interviewed on NPR's program *Fresh Air* about her book *My Life on the Road*, and it got me thinking about the Cabal again. Gloria said that one of the ways the patriarchy controls women is by controlling their reproductive rights, and therefore their bodies. She referred to a 1970s panel on abortion: "It was comprised of ten men and one nun. You can't make these things up," she said. Then she was asked about today's most pressing women's issues, and she mentioned domestic violence, female genital mutilation, rape, and sex trafficking. I kept waiting for her to mention women and weight, but she didn't.

Because it's almost always defined as a mundane matter of willpower or sloth, food gets ignored as a political issue. When Gloria was asked about her relationship with food, she mentioned her father, who weighed three hundred pounds and believed that anything could be cured by "a malted and a movie." He was sort of right about that, she said laughingly, and added that she herself still had a weakness for sweets. That was the point at which I wanted to say, wait, Gloria, you're missing something. I don't know of a single woman (and I've been privileged to be allowed entry into the inner lives of hundreds of thousands of them) who hasn't struggled with the size of her body. And when a woman's energy is tied up in judging her body, it ties up her power as well.

Might this be another way the patriarchy controls women's bodies? By hypnotizing us into believing we must be thin in order to have value, or authority? If I wanted to silence half the population of the world—the one most likely to oppose war and guns—I can't think of a better way to do it. Expecting a woman to stand up for what she knows while convincing her that she must first be thin is like binding a Chinese woman's feet and asking her to run a marathon.

We don't need a Cabal to enthrall or manipulate or silence us; we've done it ourselves (with limitless assistance of the patriarchy) by channeling most of our life's energy into having thinner thighs. This doesn't mean we should join the Fat Acceptance movement, or (only) blame men for trying to control our bodies. Even if this whole brouhaha with women, food, and weight is the patriarchy's way to silence us by keeping us focused on impossible goals (fifty women in the world look like supermodels; 3.5 billion don't, and never will), we'd still have to do the same thing: stop allowing it. When we realize we've had duct tape over our mouths for decades, there is only one thing to do: tear it off. Our power is not in blaming or shaming, but in waking up from the collective trance in which we've been living. We use the same arms we've been told are too fat, and we uncover the same mouths we've been told are too loud, and then we start telling the truth about what we already know but don't want to know we know.

There are many ways of truth-telling, but the best way I know is to ask questions and be relentlessly honest in answering them. Is it true that when I lose weight I will have the body and therefore the life I want? Have I ever lost weight? How many times? Aside from having a thinner body, did losing weight fix my relationships with friends, family, or colleagues? If it is such a cure-all, why did I gain it back? (Answers like "Because I lost my job/my spouse/ my best friend," don't count. Answers like "Yes, but next time it will be different" are excuses and probably lies.)

If there was a Cabal, or if the patriarchy was entrancing women into silence (about the destruction of the environment, the plethora of guns and mass shootings, and waging war as an answer to everything), the $60 billion weight-loss industry would be proof that they were winning. The fact that we are frightened of our hungers and our strength would be proof. And the way our energy gets trapped in dieting over and over and over again would seal the deal. (If your doctor said, "I have a cure for you but there's a ninety-nine percent chance it won't work, and I know you've tried it five or twenty times, and it saps your energy, makes you feel worthless, and keeps you stuck in the rest of your life," would you do it again? And again? And every year for as long as you live?)

When you tell the truth—when you see that as much as you *say* you want to lose weight, you are keeping it on so you don't have to engage in those parts of being alive that seem more challenging than losing weight—you can begin making different decisions about the way you spend your energy. Caroline Myss, the author of *Why People Don't Heal*, once said to me, "Imagine you have a buck of life energy to spend every day. How would you spend it?"

* * *

If your doctor said, "I have a cure for you but there's a ninety-nine percent chance it won't work, and I know you've tried it five or twenty times, and it saps your energy, makes you feel worthless, and keeps you stuck in the rest of your life," would you do it again? And again? And every year for as long as you live?

Start spending that buck differently. Start today, even for fifteen minutes. Start living as if you are already free. Skip the middleman of losing weight. Do something, anything, that brings you joy and makes you feel as if you belong here. Even for half an hour, even for fifteen minutes. If there was a Cabal or if the patriarchy was entrancing women into silence by making them feel awful about their bodies, joy and fearlessness, passion and illuminated hearts would defeat them. And the miraculous thing is that we already have those tools; we just aren't using them.

There isn't a someday. There never was. No one has ever been to the future that you keep putting your life on hold for. All we ever have is now. And if you continually put your life on hold for what your life will be like tomorrow, or next year, or when you finally lose that weight, you won't recognize that you already have what you want because you will have spent years training yourself to want, not have.

"Imagine what you could do," I often ask a group of women, "if you stop turning your energy against yourself and use it instead to question what you've been hypnotized into believing about the size of your body, and to speak up for what matters to you and your children."

"What would happen if one woman spoke the truth?" asked the poet Muriel Rukeyser. "The world would split open," she said.

Let that one be you.

> *I'd spent most of my life confused about boundaries and bodies and ownership of both.*

CHAPTER SIX

The Red String Project

The first day of my final stint in therapy, my therapist asked me to stand across the room from her. Then she started walking toward me and asked me to say "Stop!" when she got too close. When she was a few inches away, I said, "Well, maybe you could stop now."

"Are you paying attention to your body? Your center?" she asked.

"I don't have a center the way you're talking about it, and if I do, it's not talking."

She told me to think of myself as having energetic boundaries. I rolled my eyes and said that I wasn't sure people had "energetic boundaries."

"Everyone has them," she said. "When someone is talking to you and gets uncomfortably close, the discomfort is a sign that your boundary or 'personal space' has been crossed." I nodded my head, still wary but less cynical.

A few sessions later, she handed me a small ball of red string. "Sit on the floor and use the string to make a circle around yourself. Close the ends together and think of the perimeter as a boundary that no one can cross without your permission. It's your body," she said, "your personal space."

"Yeah right," I thought . . . and proceeded to cry, which, uh, burst my cynicism. "It's not really mine," I said without knowing what I was saying, and burbled on about my father and how he grabbed my butt, kissed me on the lips, treated my body as if it belonged to him. Although I'd talked about the grabbing and kissing in other therapeutic situations, my visceral reaction this time convinced me that I'd spent most of my life confused about boundaries and bodies and ownership of both. In my refusal to close the end of the circle, it was immediately clear to me that I believed the consequence of "owning" this body was losing the love on which my life depended.

"My body *isn't* mine," I repeated. "That's not how I think of it."

Like many men who fought in World War II, my father called women "broads." He thought of us as good-looking, mildly dumb, and utterly incapable of greatness. When I brought a friend from Santa Cruz to New York for Thanksgiving, he pinched her butt as we were waiting for our luggage to arrive. "As a way to say hello," he murmured with a satisfied grin, as if he'd just won a trophy for being as suave as Frank Sinatra.

Each time I put the string around myself in the following sessions, it was as if an iceberg had turned upside down and what held it in place was suddenly revealed. I'd say things like: People won't like it; I'll get in trouble; Saying no is not allowed. My past experience with my father and a variety of men over the years taught me that my body was a lure to catch their attention. If I used my body or allowed it to be used in ways that were uncomfortable, well, that was the price I needed to pay for intimacy, for connection, for belonging to the tribe. And nothing I saw or heard as I was growing up taught me otherwise. Strange men in subways sometimes masturbated when they looked at me. Other men leered and grabbed me. In my twenties and thirties, I often had sex with men before I really wanted to because I was afraid that if I didn't, they'd go away.

It took a few months and a few boxes of Kleenex before I was able to unwind the constellation of beliefs I'd inherited about my body and the feelings associated with them. To sit down in the middle of the circle, close the ends together, and say to my therapist, as she was inching her way across the floor with her string, "Don't come closer." Or "I don't want to."

*   *   *

Power is not a function of what we do, say, or achieve if it is not also connected to how we live in our physical selves.

A few years after my therapist introduced me to what I call The Red String Project I decide to try it at my next retreat. On the morning of the third day of our six-day program, a Wednesday, I hand each woman a six-foot piece of red string; I tell them to make a circle around their bodies and to join the ends of the string together. I tell them they are allowed to take up space, that it is their birthright to occupy their own bodies. Before I can finish the instructions, half the room is sobbing.

"You're wrong," Diana says. "I'm not allowed." I turn to look at her. She is tall—at least six feet—with a long auburn ponytail, freckled skin, deep-set green eyes, perhaps fifty pounds over her natural weight. She has wrapped her string so tightly around her body that it is practically under her legs. "I'll get in trouble if I close the ends," she blurts. As I am about to speak to her, I hear a nearby whisper, "I'll get in trouble if I even have a string." From the back of the room, Laurie Ann, a curly-haired, stick-thin blond woman says, "Can I have another string? One isn't enough. I need to go out in the hall, join the two strings together, and make my circle so big no one can come near."

Heads are nodding. Tears are flowing. Wads of Kleenex are being handed out.

Delilah from Australia has pink and purple cropped hair, winged black rhinestone glasses, and is wearing a gray T-shirt that says CHOCOLATE FOR PRESIDENT. She raises her hand and says, "I can't remember my father ever putting a part of him in a part of me, but then, again, he didn't have to because his hands were all over the *outside* of my body *all the time*. And he was the *good* parent. My mother was addicted to alcohol and tranquilizers and spent days in her nightgown, unable to function. If I'd ever told my father to stop touching me, I would have lost the only love I had."

They come to the retreat because they have self-identified challenges with food. They are varying degrees of overweight, normal (whatever that is), and under-weight. They are capable stay-at-home mothers, psy-chiatrists, surgeons, CEOs, therapists, singers, actors, television personalities. But give them a red string and the skyscrapers of their lives crumble like Christmas cook-ies. Give them a red string and it becomes obvious that the issue has never been food, but the ways other people have talked about, touched, and used their bodies, which in turn affects how they talk about and use their own bodies. All that happened in the moment is that (like me) they've been handed a piece of string; nothing more. But it becomes immediately apparent that most of them (and us) have unconsciously swallowed the rampant misogyny of the culture along with our mashed potatoes. This isn't a problem that only affects a small, self-selected group of retreat-going women. During the November 2016 elec-tion, Kelly Oxford requested that women use Twitter to tell stories of their first sexual assaults. *Twenty-seven mil-lion* women responded within twenty-four hours.

*   *   *

Reversing the misogyny . . .
happens first by naming the fact that
we've internalized it and now treat ourselves
with the same lack of respect as the man
who grabbed us on the subway.

We can't leapfrog into being free, unencumbered, powerful women just because we want to. Power is not a function of what we do, say, or achieve if it is not also connected to how we live in our physical selves. We can't skip the step of naming what hurt us and questioning how it distorted the ways we treat our bodies. For power to be authentic, the obstacles to it must be named. In this very moment, this means using our senses. Feeling our hands, our legs. Noticing where there is heat or coolness, pulsing or pressure. Hearing the sounds of the room. A person breathing. Bringing ourselves back to the present moment so that we have a ground upon which to notice that we are caught in the past.

True power lies in our willingness to question the beliefs we swallowed along with allowing ourselves to feel the rage at those who grabbed or touched us without permission while staying present and not acting on the desire for revenge. It's possible to feel the full range of our feelings, even hatred; we can see where they are lodged in our chests or throats or faces and we can allow them to get so big that we are towering with them and breathing fire. If then we keep sensing, feeling, allowing the effects of the past to unfold in us now, we can take ourselves back.

If we feel rather than repress or act out our rage or

hatred, the undigested feelings in our chests dissolve like a night-monster when you turn on the light. That which we could never invite into our awareness because it was too big or too furious or too horrible becomes the source of our power and the guide to effective, authentic action.

Hatred is a scary word, a scary feeling for most people and so we repress it. Or we imagine what would happen if we acted it out: we'd go on a killing rampage; we'd play high-speed bumper cars with the driver who just cut us off; we'd slice off someone's head without blinking; we'd wring the neck of the neighbor's dog that whined all night. At its core, hatred is the desire to annihilate that which is causing us pain, in the misguided belief that if we could only incinerate what seems to be causing the pain, we would finally be at peace. All feuds, all wars, all acts of revenge are built on this principle, including our inner war with food and weight.

⋆　　⋆　　⋆

On diets, we are still relying on the big powerful other to know what's best and to save us. And whether it's a good daddy or a good diet that rescues us, we remain victims and food our perpetrator.

At my last retreat, many people were furious at my suggestion that they could question the link between the beliefs that resulted from being touched inappropriately and their compulsive eating. One woman said, "I don't like this approach of questioning stories and beliefs. It feels mean and lacking in compassion. My uncle raped me for three years and although I've been working on this in therapy for twenty years, I'm not over it yet— I feel as if you're telling me it's time to let go of something I'm not ready to let go of."

A slippery slope indeed. To be clear: I am not asking anyone to let go of anything, least of all fury or hatred. It's impossible to will yourself to let go of such huge and sticky feelings. I am asking that we feel what we feel instead of think what we feel. Reversing the misogyny of our culture is an inside job. It happens first by naming the fact that we've internalized it and now treat ourselves with the same lack of respect as the man who grabbed us on the subway.

Because it's a lifeless strand and not a present-day situation, because we are acting as if our mothers or fathers or teachers or random men are in the room when many of them are dead and the rest aren't in the room, the red string allows people to see that the immediate reactions they are wedded to are from the past. Which means that embedded in the extra weight we carry around is an unconscious attitude about women's bodies we've inherited. Freeing ourselves from this body-hatred means naming the misogyny we've internalized.

The most challenging part of respecting our bodies and healing compulsive eating is the conscious decision to question what keeps us bound and silenced. Until we can sit in our own skin and fully occupy the physical space we've been given, we will be apologetic about our bodies. And even when we lose weight because we stuck to a diet, we will remain frightened of ourselves because we know that it's the diet that's keeping us thin, not our own capacity to stay true to what we know or want. On diets, we are still relying on the big powerful other to know what's best and to save us. And whether it's a good daddy or a good diet that rescues us, we remain victims and food our perpetrator.

For a few months after we complete The Red String Project (which takes repeated practice), some of my students carry their strings in their pockets and imagine putting it around them when they talk to their mothers, fathers, bosses. Many of them make bracelets out of a narrow strand of red leather so they have a visual touchstone of what they've learned. Both are concrete reminders that they can take back their body from the beliefs and people who snatched it, and reclaim the capacity to say no, or yes, or not now. They become centered in their power. Their actions in the world become effective, not reactive. Some students have become political leaders in their hometowns. One works with battered women. Almost all of them realize that although their own mothers did not have the needed understanding to stop rampant body-abuse, they do—and they can teach their daughters what they themselves never learned. First there is one of us, then fifty, then a hundred and fifty. Soon we will be a crowd, two hundred thousand, twenty-seven million. We are saying no and we are saying yes, and whether we whisper or shout, we are saying it together. I can hear you.

*In the world you
cannot see, touch, eat,
losing weight and joy
are unrelated.*

CHAPTER SEVEN

In the End

In the end, the point of losing weight is not to lose
weight. It's not to get into a pair of size six jeans,
eat chocolate every day, or have cantaloupe buns. Which
isn't to say that any or all of these aren't sublime here
on the physical plane where we muddle around day after
day: they are. But in the world you cannot see, touch,
eat, losing weight and joy are unrelated.

Everyone who has lost weight knows this, but we
keep forgetting it when we gain weight so that we can

once again look forward to an imaginary happy future. Also, participating in the cycle of judging and shaming ourselves followed by feeling accomplished and elated gives us something to do and talk about, a way to pass the time. There's nothing wrong with this pattern; it's how our minds work. We intuitively understand that we want something we cannot see or touch, but we don't know how to name or access it. And so we fall back into believing that being thinner will right everything that is wrong. The only problem is that it's based on a lie.

The first time I caught on to the lie, I was twenty-eight. I'd just gained eighty pounds in two months, effectively doubling my weight after having spent a few years as an eighty-two-pound anorexic. The fattest I'd ever been, I finally realized I'd been thin many times and it had never fulfilled its promise—and that the emphasis on body size was a hoax. The next morning, I started on a two-week regimen of eating raw chocolate chip cookies punctuated with daily doses of Polar Bear pumpkin ice cream. I figured that if being thinner wasn't going to make me happy, and if depriving and shaming myself had no benefit, why do it? Why not eat cookie dough instead? This is how many of us spend our lives. Eating the equivalent of cookie dough, then dieting, then eating cookie dough, then dieting. We understand in a remote part of ourselves that we want something we cannot see or touch, but we don't know how to name or access it. And so we fall back into believing that being thinner will right everything that is wrong.

———— ✬ ————

Modern dancer and choreographer Martha Graham wrote, "There is a vitality, a life force, an energy, a quickening that is translated through you into action, and because there is only one of you in all of time, this expression is unique. And if you block it, it will never exist through any other medium, and be lost. The world will not have it. It is not your business to determine how good it is, nor how valuable, nor how it compares with other expressions. It is your business to keep it yours clearly and directly, to keep the channel open." Since that uniqueness needs a vehicle of expression, and since the vehicle we've been given is our body, we do what we can to keep the channel open. When you stuff or starve it, your body shuts down. It cannot reveal its purpose or creativity or wisdom to you. Also, no one wants to listen to a burping, farting channel.

It's uncomfortable to walk around in a body that is uncomfortable. It's hard to let innate brilliance or power express itself when you are schlepping around twenty or fifty extra pounds. It's not impossible, just more difficult. And since there is already so much inherent difficulty in being alive, what with people getting sick, raising kids, dying, and the earth on the verge of destruction, why not make life easier on yourself? Why not make the effort to discover what enhances your aliveness and vitality? Because when you do, you become less and less fascinated with those foods, activities, and people that don't.

* * *

We intuitively understand that we want something we cannot see or touch, but we don't know how to name or access it. And so we fall back into believing that being thinner will right everything that is wrong. The only problem is that it's based on a lie.

In my mind there is only one true reason to lose weight: to keep the channel open. You think the pain is about the twenty pounds that's separating you from fitting into your jeans, but that's the crux of the lie, as all those people on their deathbeds will tell you. (Google people, regrets, deathbeds, and read about the five, twenty-seven, or thirty-five things they say; their regrets, without exception, are about allowing themselves to get distracted by some form of the lie.) The Indian sage Nisargadatta writes that all teachings, "whatever their source . . . , have only one aim: to save you from the calamity of a separate existence—of being a meaningless dot in a vast and beautiful picture."

In some part of ourselves, we know this. We know that what we're doing on this earth is manifesting spirit in the only physical vehicle we've been given—our body; by doing so we're saving ourselves from the calamity of leaving the earth without showing up. Eventually, we become more dedicated to keeping the channel open than to eating meat loaf when we are not hungry. And although we keep faltering, keep slipping, keep being seduced by the lie, one day we will be more drawn to the truth than to the endless fascination with drama, pretty things, and thinner thighs.

The only best reason to do this—to keep the channel open—is that there, in that vast space, we find love itself, flagrant, unstinting, give-it-all-away love. Not just for our spouses or children or particular community, but for arms and legs and nights and fog, love for the mornings, floors, caterpillars, and trees. Love for the sounds your foot makes on the sidewalk, for traffic and honking horns, for the earth itself. Nothing is left out. Zen teachers call it discovering "your original face." We do whatever it takes to keep the channel open because when we don't, it hurts, and when we do, it doesn't. Also, there is nothing better to do with a life.

PART TWO

Through
the Mind

> *Living on the inside*
> *of my mind—or rather,*
> *believing the things my mind*
> *regales me with regularly—*
> *is like chewing nails.*

CHAPTER EIGHT

Zen Mind, Puppy Mind

We adopted a puppy last week and it hasn't been pretty around here. Well, really, it hasn't been pretty *in* here. My mind, that is. Izzy the puppy, however, is pretty. She looks like a stuffed toy. Big brown eyes and a nose like a plump olive. Red fur that is soft and a bit curly. My friend Catherine says she looks like a person impersonating Lucille Ball. Cute little puppy running around with her black "Pawda" stuffed purse. From the outside, you'd think that our house was the picture of adorableness. Then you might take a look at my face and see that there's trouble in paradise.

Izzy was a sort of rescue dog. "Sort of" because she wasn't supposed to be a rescue; my husband and I aren't that virtuous. I know, I know, it's terrible, and if I had a tail, it would be between my legs. Good-hearted people, people who care about the earth, do not buy dogs. I, however, am not one of those people. Don't get me wrong. I give money every year to Save a Sato, the Marin Humane Society, and Best Friends Animal Sanctuary. I believe that the people who save dogs and the people who adopt those dogs are angels.

I, it must now be apparent, am not an angel. Plus, almost everyone I know who has adopted rescue dogs— okay, three people (none of my other friends are silly enough to even get a dog, and I understand their feelings much more this week than last week)—told us that it's taken two years for their dogs to stop submission-peeing and fear-biting. I don't want to wait two years. I'm already sixty-five; I don't want to spend the time I have left, not even two years of it, with a submissively peeing dog.

So, we decided to buy a puppy—a four-legged fluff of jubilation. We looked at a litter of nine, all of which were like those irresistible puppies you see on YouTube. All, that is, except for one that was cowering in the corner. She was shaking and frightened and couldn't get away from the bully that kept attacking her. She wouldn't walk over to us. She wouldn't make eye contact with us. And in a moment of weakness, a moment of remembering what it felt like to be the chubby kid who never got picked for soccer but did get picked on by Peter Zimmerman, the class bully, my heart melted. And so, when Matt said, "If we don't take her, I don't think anyone else will," I agreed.

Until last week I would have told you that I like animals more than people. "I am an animal person," I say, when people start talking about babies and puppies. After it rains, I spend hours saving salamanders and frogs from getting run over. The hummingbirds in my backyard land on my fingers. And I, who abhor being wet or cold, have been known to jump into icy bodies of water to save drowning baby birds. I fancy myself like Clarissa Estés, in *Women Who Run with the Wolves*. I could be wild enough to run with (very nice) wolves, or at least capable of loping with a poodle. (Izzy, by the way, is a standard poodle.) But today I am not an animal person. Today I don't like anything on four legs, especially the one that looks like Lucille Ball.

I blame my husband. He, Matt, is the one who wanted a dog. And not just any dog. He wanted a girl dog. A big nonshedding girl dog—and this is the important part—that was related (through a complicated series of blood lines) to Celeste, our dog that died a year ago. Me? I was enjoying not having a pet for the first time in eighteen years. Enjoying being able to walk out the door and not see those big eyes staring at me through the window, silently accusing me of abandonment. But Matt also has big doggy eyes, and when he looked at me ever so sweetly and said, "I really want a dog now," I caved in.

I'm usually not a pushover, but—and I say this in the kindest possible way—Matt is very doglike. Every morning he greets me like he hasn't seen me for ten years. "Hi sweetheart," he says brightly. Big smile. Crinkly eyes, like the sun is just now rising and using his face as its stage. Sometimes I am glum, introverted, and rather dramatic—sort of like Isadora Duncan (was her nickname Izzy?), who was strangled to death by her own scarf. So as Matt walked around shaking off sparks of light while telling me how much he wanted a puppy, I thought, well, it doesn't seem right to deprive him, and anyway, why not get a dog? I am, after all, an animal person.

But today I am convinced we made a huge mistake. Izzy walks around (when she's willing to come out from under the bed) with her tail down, afraid of everything—doorways, stuffed toys, food, water, friends, Matt, me. Last week, a woman who started a sanctuary for abused and abandoned dogs came over to help bring Izzy out of her shell. After three hours she said, "Your dog is as bad as any feral dog I've met." This from a person who rescues dogs thrown over bridges in Mexico City. This from the woman who drives around with ten feral dogs in her car, most of whom look like large rats.

*   *   *

For the longest time I clung to the conviction that scary thoughts are created by scary situations: . . . I couldn't tell the difference between my stories of a situation and the situation itself.

If I was going to get a dog, I'd say to my husband— and apparently the "if" part of that sentence is now moot—I want a dog that's happy. I want a dog that could remind me that day-to-day joy is possible. I tell him about my friend Nina's nephew who spent a year searching for a puppy, adopted one, and within a week decided he wasn't cut out to be a puppy father. I tell him the story of the writer Joyce Maynard who adopted two girls from Ethiopia, soon realized it was a mistake, and gave them back (i.e., found them a home with two stable parents). If people can give back their children, I tell Matt, I can give back a puppy. Can we please just FedEx Izzy back to where she came from?

But, and I am now going to get to the point of this story, I began to see that living on the inside of my mind—or rather, believing the things my mind regales me with regularly—is like chewing nails. For instance, the night before I married Matt, I was convinced I was gay and was marrying a man because I lacked the courage to come out. Twelve hours before walking down the aisle, I was suddenly beset with memories of my wild attraction to Rose Koven in eighth grade and the downy pleasure of feeling each other's breasts (which were a bit like large mosquito bites) on the orange pillows in my bedroom. After confiding this to my friend Sil, she reminded me that although I'd had many opportunities to be with women since eighth grade, I really did prefer the smell and feel of men, particularly the one I was marrying the next day.

For the longest time I clung to the conviction that scary thoughts are created by scary situations: losing someone you love; being fired; having your house burn down; being diagnosed with a terminal illness. I couldn't tell the difference between my stories of a situation and the situation itself. When I believe my stories I am convinced I'm living the wrong life, and I've found that without the stories there is a simplicity and an elegance to life as it is unfolding in this very moment.

With Izzy—because the stakes are, er, somewhat lower than marrying a person of the wrong sex or being diagnosed with a terminal illness—I see that although having a dog whose nervous system reminds me of my own wouldn't be my first choice, there is something about this dog that I feel as if I already know. Almost, but not exactly, as if I'd been waiting for her and there she was, but not in the dog costume I was expecting.

Therefore, with uncharacteristic maturity I have made a promise to stop myself whenever I notice I am listening to the stories my mind prattles on about. Since I could switch the Izzy story with many similar tales I've told myself that were not true, it has once again become quite clear to me that, as spiritual teacher Catherine Ingram says, the mind is mad. When I remind myself of that, I don't take the thoughts that I need a different dog/life/husband personally.

The truth is that along with its multiple and exhilarating pleasures, there is something deeply uncomfortable about being human. About loving for the sake of it, even when you know that everything and everyone you love is going to get lost, get broken, or die—particularly four-legged beings that almost always die before you.

When I first met Matt he was grieving the loss of his previous partner, who'd been diagnosed with ovarian cancer six months after they met, and died five years later. Despite knowing her for only 182 days (I counted), he accompanied her through four and a half years of chemotherapy treatments, hair losses, excruciating pain, three remissions, and the dying process. But you'd just met, I thought. How could you willingly go through that kind of heartbreak and loss? Why didn't you just leave? (Never mind that after knowing him for twenty minutes, I felt as if I could go swimming in the ocean of his heart, it was that big. Or that when I heard he stayed with his partner, I realized that he was a man who loved with fierceness and loyalty—and I liked that, even if I didn't understand it.) When I finally asked him why he stayed, he said he understood that the pain of losing her would be so much less than the pain of never having loved her at all.

As the weeks have rolled along, the situation with Izzy has changed, as situations always do. She's kissing us now, puts her wet-truffle nose in the crook of my neck every morning to be nuzzled. Despite my reluctance, I find myself laughing at her prance-prance-leap before she picks up a toy, and the crossing of her paws when she lies down, as if awaiting high tea and scones.

The way she lives in the world, as any animal person knows, is a portal to what the Zen masters call Beginner's Mind.

Everything is new to her, even the scent of the redwood tree she's passed a few hundred times; despite her hypervigilant nervous system, she is a constant reminder that although I've seen the tree in our driveway, the succulents in our garden, the helicopter-flight of the hummingbirds a hundred thousand times, I haven't seen them *today*.

And according to Zen masters and dogs, there *is* no other day. No one has ever touched or experienced the future because, when it arrives, it is still only today—which makes it a perfect day to revel in the spectacle of being aboveground, and throwing a pink elephant toy across the room dozens of first times.

★　　★　　★

Although I've seen the tree in our driveway, the succulents in our garden, the helicopter-flight of the hummingbirds a hundred thousand times, I haven't seen them **today.**

> *Each of us plays host
> to at least two or three distinct
> identities that when triggered
> feel utterly familiar. They feel
> like who we actually are.*

CHAPTER NINE

Be Kind to the Ghost Children

Izzy has an eating disorder. When I put her food bowl down, she looks at me as if it's a couch, as if the fact that she is supposed to eat it hasn't occurred to her. My cat, Blanche, also had a problem with food: he was so fat that when he sat on your head in the middle of the night, you felt as if your brain was being crushed. And there was Celeste, our dog before Izzy, who was allergic to dog food, and could only eat white rice, chicken breast, and egg yolks for the first three years of her life. No, it has not escaped my purview that one hundred percent of the animals that live with me manifest extreme food symptoms.

Matt and I take Izzy to a vet that my friend Annie tells me about. She says Rob-the-vet is a miracle worker. She also says that coincidentally all of her animals have had eating disorders, too (she puts *coincidentally* in capital letters), and tells me that Rob-the-vet worked with Koko-the-gorilla. At the mention of Koko, I swoon. Although I have tried to visit Koko in Palo Alto for years—she adopted a homeless kitten and was friends with Robin Williams—I have not been able to arrange a meeting.

Rob-the-vet has startling ice-blue eyes and palomino hair that drifts like crazy wings down his collar. On his walls are the requisite letters from kids written in big crayon rainbow colors: "Dear Dr. Rob, Thank you for saving Lucy. She wasn't feeling so good, love, Miranda." "Dear Dr. Rob, Even though Bongo has one eye, I love him better than my brother. Thank you for helping him, love, Mandy." During our first session Rob tells us that Izzy, who is a year and a half, has no belly center. Actually he says, "She has no abdomen content." She is in the throes of a shock pattern from being abused, attacked, and bullied for the first twelve weeks of her life—which, according to him, are the most formative.

Then Rob proceeds with his specialty: the "psychomotor treatment," which consists of different kinds of massages—on her spine, in her joints, on her head—coupled with looking deep into Izzy's eyes and holding her close to his belly. "Do you want to try it?" he asks us. I nod, then look at Matt to see if he'd like to go first, but since relaxing is not a challenge for him, he has taken this opportunity to nap.

Rob asks me to stand belly to belly with him and to breathe. Although it does feel somewhat comforting to lean against a big belly, what gets to me, what really makes an impression, is that he keeps emphasizing that Izzy will be fine, that she can learn to regulate herself, and that it is me who needs to relax.

"Are you a nice person?" he asks me.

I am about to launch into the many ways in which I am cranky and selfish when Rob says, "I don't really need to know the circumstances in which you aren't nice, just a general impression of whether you are kind to your animals."

I nod and tell him that my teacher Jeanne says that in her next life she is coming back as my dog. Rob says, "Then she has enough of what she needs—food, water, space to run, kindness—and she will be fine. Relax," he says. "She will discover her own relationship with food, but you have to hold the line. You can't let her manipulate you with those big eyes and her history of abuse and abandonment."

Now he's talking.

I am a sucker for tales of abuse and abandonment, mine and others. Being abused served me in many ways (although I would not have chosen it), and it gave me a story to tell in my first few books. (Also, writing about people who hurt you is an excellent way to take revenge, but only people who aren't nice would know that.) And it provided the longing to see what, if anything, lay beyond a life of drowning myself in fried chicken and coffee ice cream.

"Because," Rob continues, "she has been living with you for a year and a half now—many times longer than the three months in which she was abused—and being frightened of food or people means she is living in the past, not the present. Unless you muster equal parts kindness and fierceness with her, the stance of having being abused—and what she is able to get from you because of it—will become a way of life."

I am listening intently but can no longer figure out whether he is talking about Izzy or me. Because although abuse and how I used food to dull its pain became a portal for me, it also provided a solid identity of being The Wounded One Who Survived. Having spent years in therapy and written books about what happened, there is a teeny chance that I began wearing the wounds as adornments, as my calling card. "You think you had it tough? You think you had a difficult childhood? Read my book *When Food Is Love* and get back to me."

Rob interrupts my thoughts and says, "I think I can help her. Come once a week for six weeks, and let's see how it goes."

As I've worked with my students about what happens in the moment before they eat compulsively, I've come to realize that each of us plays host to at least two or three distinct identities that when triggered feel utterly familiar. They feel like who we actually are. We feel rejected or sad or lonely—and, in a flash, we shape-shift. Then we begin telling ourselves stories. *This always happens. They always leave. I will always be alone. I need to eat.* And because we've told ourselves those same things for many years, we believe they are true; the familiarity of the feelings, and the fact that they keep repeating themselves in many different situations, means, it seems, that the stories, and who we take ourselves to be in them, are who we really are.

In my retreat work we call these historical, familiar identities the ghost children. Some of us—most of us—don't just have one ghost child; we have a series of well-worn but incredibly painful selves whose skins we inhabit as easily as we slip on old, ratty coats from the back of the closet. Some of us (I won't mention names) are running day-care centers for ghost children. Listening to, and believing, these voices, is partly responsible for the urge to eat when we are not hungry.

One of my retreat students is sobbing. She has been in a relationship for six months with someone, she says, who loves her. She says it is the first time in her life—she is thirty-two—that she is loving and being loved by someone who doesn't abuse her. When I saw her six months ago, before she met her lover, she looked vibrant and joyful. Now, she says, all she can do is eat. And eat.

"I come home from work every night and I walk straight to the refrigerator. I open it. I dive into it as if it was my last chance at survival. Then I spend the night bingeing." Through a gush of tears, she tells me that "All I know of love is loss."

"Really?" I ask. "All you know is loss?"

"Yes," she says, and cries louder, harder.

We both know that what she is saying isn't true, because in order to have survived this long she would have needed what psychologists call "good-enough love." We also know that she has spent five months being with someone who understands and cherishes her. But her experience at this moment is subsumed by a ghost child. By the one who was abused, the one who wasn't seen or cherished. And although there are many feelings that have become associated with love— loss, fear, abuse, shame, abandonment—they are not true in this moment. Nonetheless, those feelings are present and it is not helpful to push them away, or tell her to snap out of it and grow herself up. But neither would it serve her to believe that what she is saying is true.

After a while, the stories from our past begin to feel like poems we memorized in fifth grade, or Beatles songs we learned by heart. They evoke memories, feelings, possibilities or the lack of them, and if we believe them we are defined by them. It's as if we draw a circle around ourselves and say, This is me. This is what

I am capable of. This is how it will be forever. Instead of being kind to the ghost children, instead of treating them as Rob urged me to treat Izzy (with a combination of kindness toward the pain and fierceness about not being manipulated by it), we either try to get rid of them or we become them. Either way, it's like living on the inside of a scream from twenty, thirty, fifty years ago.

Another story from a retreat: It is eight a.m., breakfast time, and more than a hundred of us are gathered in the dining room of the retreat center. The room is steamy and hot from bodies and coffee and mounds of scrambled eggs. Thirteen tables of eight fill the room; I stand on the side, ready to speak to anyone who is curious about the amount or kind of food she has put on her plate. Since most of us use food in secret by rationalizing why, just this once, we deserve to have this pancake/cinnamon bun/cake otherwise we will die, being in a crowded room with your plate piled with food and being asked to pay attention is like wearing your insides on the outside. There is nowhere to hide.

A woman named Barrie raises her hand. She has large

brown eyes, short cropped gray hair, and is perhaps seventy-five pounds over her natural weight. I weave my way through the space between the chairs, and stand beside her right shoulder. She starts to cry immediately, stops after a few moments, and looks down at her plate. It is piled high with eggs, three pieces of toast, mounds of potatoes, and two cinnamon buns.

"I've taken enough food to feed three people," she says.

"Yes," I say, "it seems you have. I wonder who or what you are feeding."

Without missing a beat, she says, "My mother died this year and I miss her so much I can't stand it. The grief is too much. It's too much." She starts to cry again. Then she says, "I tried taking my cat for a walk on a leash, and he didn't want to go, so he just bent over, laid on the ground, and wouldn't get up. I feel like my cat. I don't want to get up. I just want to eat."

I ask Barrie how old she feels.

"Ten years old and I've lost my mom and there's nothing I can do to bring her back. I can't handle this by myself. I'll fall apart if I let myself feel it."

"And what will food do?"

"Fill the hole left by my mom."

"And how's that working?" I ask.

She stops crying and a giggle escapes. "Not so well. I've gained forty pounds and my mom hasn't come back. I'm afraid I'll get swallowed by the grief so I keep eating to make it go away."

"And now?" I ask. "What about right now?"

"Now I feel sad . . ."

"Where in your body do you feel that?" I ask.

"In my chest. In my stomach. It feels heavy, like a dark, dense cloud."

"And what happens if you stay with the feelings instead of pushing them away by eating?"

"Well," she answers, "when I feel the sadness itself, it feels dark but also soft. It feels heavy but also warm. I don't feel like my cat anymore, I just feel heavy, warm, soft, and dark. But I also feel something else: a tenderness toward it."

"And the food on your plate? How do you feel about that?"

"Like it could feed me and a small army. Like I don't want it anymore."

People come to my retreats to get rid of their issues with food. They want peace. They want release. And they want it by the end of the weeklong retreat. I understand the urgency; I know that what they really want—and it does feel urgent—is to be free from what tortures them. From all the voices that tell them they're not good enough. From what prompts them to eat when they are not hungry. From the suffering of a lifetime.

I was waiting most of my life for that. And I believed, really believed, that the freedom and the joy I imagined would come with it existed as a destination, like a balmy tropical island where Brazilian bikini waxes were outlawed, and piña coladas were free. If only I could skip over the painful parts. If only I wasn't myself.

Just last week I was back to thrashing around in ghost stories ("I'm a failure; I'm dying of cancer of something that hasn't yet been discovered; I'm too needy, my needs are repulsive") and the feelings that accompany them: depression, emptiness, and loneliness. I call it my Pigpen state. (According to Peanuts, "Pigpen travels in his own private dust storm knowing full well that he has affixed to him the dust of ages.") The next day, I realized that I was swinging between two familiar poles: moping around in my own private dust storm and losing patience with the moping. Then I remembered that this process of discovery used to take weeks, and I also recalled that I can make a choice: I can decide to step out of my stories and turn toward the feelings directly.

Turning toward myself in that moment feels like the very opposite of what any normal person would do (which is to run, screaming, in the opposite direction and toward the ice cream). It feels like I am choosing to die. And in some ways, I am because when I turn toward myself, the old-me story dissolves.

★   ★   ★

For many reasons, we could not feel the hurt or pain or abandonment at the time it arose— twenty or thirty or fifty years ago—so we keep feeling it now in the form of frightened, ashamed, unlovable ghost children. The choice now is whether we keep believing in, and reinforcing, those images in our minds, or whether we stop.

The gaggle of ghost children—the worthlessness and shame and beliefs about how I/we should be, could be, should have been—are based on elaborate stories about why what happened, happened. For many reasons, we could not feel the hurt or pain or abandonment at the time it arose—twenty or thirty or fifty years ago—so we keep feeling it now in the form of frightened, ashamed, unlovable ghost children. The choice now is whether we keep believing in, and rein-forcing, those images in our minds, or whether we stop. Whether we retreat into old stories each time we feel rejected or whether we turn toward that well of beliefs and the pain that accompanies them and allow them to speak. This turning toward is the very defini-tion of kindness.

When, on that Pigpen morning of my discontent, I stopped clenching against the pain (i.e., believing my thoughts about how awful I was), I remembered an interaction I'd had a few days before, with a friend who seemed to be withdrawing from our relationship—and I slowly realized I was blaming myself for wanting too much. And since a version of that interaction hap-pened many times over many years—*Why do you always need, need, need? Can't you think of anyone but yourself?*—I began seeing myself the way I believed other people saw me: as repulsive, as wanting too much, as an open wound.

That morning I decided that instead of being disgusted by Pigpen, I'd invite him in. And then. Everything hurt. My skin, my feet, my chest. Without my mind's stories about the hurt—Oh my God, this will never end; what if I can't ever get off the bed?—it became a red pulsing sensation in the back of my chest. And as I allowed it to be there, it changed; first it softened, and then it spread like a wave into my arms, and down my belly. Tears came. I could feel my childhood confusion, the way I shrank to fit the space I thought my family could tolerate. And then came tenderness. For the child who couldn't get enough of her mother, and for the mother who couldn't take being wanted by her child. For the situation itself.

＊　　＊　　＊

Each time we turn toward rather than away from ourselves, the part of ourselves that is not our story arises.

"Poor Pigpen," I thought. And in that moment, I wasn't young and I wasn't old. I wasn't crazy and I wasn't lonely. I was both the pain and that which was holding the pain. The sadness and that which was noticing the sadness. The unlove and that which was untouched by the lack of love. Stillness itself.

All any feeling wants is to be welcomed with tenderness. It wants room to unfold. It wants to relax and tell its story. And the magic of this is that each time we turn toward rather than away from ourselves, the part of ourselves that is not our story arises.

Spiritual teachers call that which has never, not for one second, been affected by anything that has ever happened, true nature or presence of God. It is ageless and pure, responsive and full of potential. And what it feels like, what it always feels like, is that the noise in our minds has stopped. And for what may be the first time (or the five thousandth time, it doesn't matter), anything is possible. We are free.

It always feels the same, the turn that happens when I realize I've been in the thrall of an entity using my body as its host but now I have a choice about whether to free myself from its clutches. "Really?" I think. "I'm allowed to do this? There is no prison, no door, no key? Really?"

CHAPTER TEN

Hoodwinked by Suffering

A few years ago, my friend Michael had his prostate removed, which meant he was bedridden with a catheter up his penis and a urine bag attached to his hip. From his bed, he told me that because he'd been doing tai chi and chi gong for thirty years, he had just created a new kind of "laying-down tai chi," and was healing much faster than the doctor expected. He waved his hands over his pelvis a few times to demonstrate. "You do look radiant for someone who's just had surgery," I replied—and he did.

As my husband, Matt, and I were driving home, It started:

I can't believe I didn't follow through with that chi gong practice. What is WRONG with me?

What if I have to have my ovaries removed and I don't know how to wave my hands over their absence and heal myself?

I KNEW I should have taken up tai chi thirty years ago when everyone was flying to Hawaii and studying with Al What's-His-Name. Now it's too late. I blew it. Again.

Along with—and even more pronounced than—the Greek chorus of judgments was the set of physical reactions that accompanied It: a pounding heart; a stomach that felt as if it had fallen through my feet and taken my legs with it; a sense of having withered and shrunk. Then came the wave of emotional reactions to the physical reactions: a feeling of irrevocable failure; desperation to climb out of myself; neediness for "a big person" to rescue flailing me. And, as if that wasn't enough, reactions to the original judgments started piling up:

You're such a fraud. You're supposed to be teaching other people how to disengage from this mess and you can't even do it yourself. How many times, for how many years, are you going to have to keep going through this? Don't you ever learn?

Then, the final insult (which seems to be a favorite,

although it often has nothing to do with the situation at hand): *You are going to die fat, miserable, and alone, with moles on your face that have bristles sticking out.*

In the car, we were passing fields of grazing cows, humps of ocher hills dotted with wind-twisted shrubs and sprawling trees. Matt was burbling about how well Michael seemed and hadn't yet realized that she who had woken up with him, left the house with him, walked in Michael's door with him, had disappeared in a whorl of comparative judgment and shame. When I didn't respond to his attempts at conversation, he turned and said, "Are you okay, sweetheart?"

Silence.

What I really wanted to say was "No, and would it be okay if I walked into your body now so that I could leave mine? And if that's not a possibility, would you mind telling me ten or a hundred reasons why you love me because I can't remember a single reason why you should."

But I didn't want to tell Matt the truth. I didn't want him to discover that I'd been pulling the wool over his eyes for thirty years and that he'd married an impostor. So I lied to him instead.

"Sorry," I answered. "Yes, Michael looked great and isn't the pink sky gorgeous and are we having poached salmon for dinner or did we decide on that zucchini frittata with chard from the garden?"

By morning, I was still feeling small and panicky. Over breakfast of grilled cheese on sourdough toast with avocados and tomatoes, I murmured, "I should have taken up tai chi years ago when everyone was doing it; I missed my chance." And Matt, having spent years listening to my laments about the life I could have had if only I hadn't been myself, responded, "Uh, isn't that the bully?" and added: "The voice of what Catherine Ingram calls 'the crazy aunt in the attic'?"

"Hmm," I said, "maybe." And then I dismissed the crazy-aunt possibility and thought, "He loves me too much to see how damaged I am. Or else, he's too lazy to get a divorce." But as I finished the last bite of avocado, I started feeling like Patty Duke playing Helen Keller.

In the movie *The Miracle Worker*, Anne Sullivan, Helen's teacher, refuses to let her leave the table until she understands the connection between the egg she is eating and the word for it. Despite Helen's tantrums, Anne persists with signing the word into her hand until finally Helen makes a connection between two things that were previously unrelated—and "a new light comes into her face." When Matt named the bully-aunt dynamic, I was able to see the connection between the doom and its cause; I saw that whenever the bully is around, the needy panicky one is also around, that they are a duo. And I saw that they were actually just thought patterns and I didn't need to believe them.

It always feels the same, the turn that happens when I realize I've been in the thrall of an entity using my body as its host but now I have a choice about whether to free myself from its clutches. "Really?" I think. "I'm allowed to do this? There is no prison, no door, no key? Really?" Seeing that I *can* free myself *is* freeing myself since the awareness noticing the struggle is outside of it, and therefore already free from it. And being on the other side of comparative judgment or shame always, every single time, feels exultingly light, as if I've gone to the closet, put on the wings that were hanging beside my puffer coat, and am now soaring around treetops, shouting Hallelujah at every red-tailed hawk I pass.

Each engagement with the aunt has recognizable ingredients: a big know-it-all wagging its finger at a small whimpering ghost child.

The trigger can be anything at all: something someone says or does, a situation at work, an article about George Clooney or Annie Dillard, visiting a friend. You start comparing yourself to your own expectations of what you thought was going to happen and didn't or who you thought you were going to become and haven't.

Triggers are personal and conditioned by your history and vulnerabilities (i.e., Matt did not respond to visiting Michael the way I did); *they do not have to do with the situation itself*. No one can cause you to compare, shrink, or shame yourself; a trigger is created when you believe your thoughts and the feelings they evoke.

The physical reaction to the trigger: the pounding heart, the sinking chest, the feeling of shrinking to pint size. The sensation of energy draining from your body and leaving emptiness in its place, of being paralyzed or just too little to deal with this big bad world.

The emotional reaction to the trigger (which is often simultaneous with the physical reaction): feeling small, young, abandoned, incapable, lost or unloved, doomed or dumb, isolated or valueless. Or all of the above. Although the trigger doesn't create particular thoughts or feelings or judgments, it does catalyze latent parts that have not been fully felt or understood. Everyone's got those parts—it's impossible to be born into this human, vulnerable body and escape unscathed—and until we meet them with compassion and openness, we are lived by them; they are who we take ourselves to be.

* * *

No one can cause you to compare,
shrink, or shame yourself; a trigger is
created when you believe your thoughts
and the feelings they evoke.

The bully-aunt seemingly comes to the rescue by telling you what you should or could have done to avoid feeling this way now. Its main message is: "If only you had done that, then you wouldn't be feeling this." And: "There is only one way to live, I know that way, and you are doing it wrong." Unfortunately, we don't hear the judgments as if they are coming from the bully; we hear them in the first person as proclamations of truth, as if they are coming from a wiser, better, all-knowing part of ourselves.

If I had taken up tai chi, I wouldn't be feeling so afraid or doomed. And I could heal myself if I got cancer.

If I hadn't decided to start my own business, I wouldn't be terrified of not having enough money now.

If only I had lost ten pounds, I would be in a relationship now and not be so lonely.

In each circumstance, the bully is shouting an under-lying, deeper criticism from the wings:

You didn't take up tai chi because you're lazy and now your health will be ruined.

You are worried about having enough money? Well, guess what? It serves you right for believing you could start your own business.

You're fat because you are sloth with no willpower; no wonder you're not in a relationship.

Ouch.

Engaging with this voice is like mud wrestling with a pig, which never ends well, since the outcome is always the same: "You both get dirty and the pig likes it" (says George Bernard Shaw).

Over the years, I've tried and taught a variety of disengagements: defending myself by saying go away or fuck you; listing the crazy aunt's attacks by writing them down in the third person; thanking it for trying to protect me by shutting me down and, therefore, keeping me from making further mistakes. But the only one that has ever truly worked is awareness itself: noticing that I feel as if the ground has suddenly fallen away and I am living the wrong life; at that point, even if it is days later, I can backtrack, name the trigger, notice its accompanying sensations, and question the doom to which I've been wedded.

But—and here's the snag—since most of us believe (and are afraid not to believe) the criticisms leveled at us from an inner bully, we also believe that being loved and/or having the life we envision means obeying the One That Knows how to do it, have it, be it. So, although we may be peripherally aware that we feel as if we've shrunk, we are convinced that this-that-we-are-now is our true self, and we are back where we belong.

Disengaging from this voice requires a willingness to consider that we've spent our lives hoodwinked by suffering, and that it's possible to be free. This, in turn, requires a willingness to see that what most of us call "me-myself-I" ricochets from one insane voice in our head to another.

Choosing not to believe the crazy aunts is like choosing not to diet; it's radical, frightening, and exhilarating because, let's face it, it's comforting to have a voice in your head that is absolutely certain about what's wrong and what's right, as well as what you need to do and eat to be loved, safe, and successful. And since most of us prefer to have company than be alone, we don't question our loyalty to these decades-old instructions or the fact that we often find ourselves wandering in the twilight zone of worthlessness and despair. We keep choosing to stay loyal to our past and our parents' instructions rather than to be free.

It takes courage to question our comparative judgments because we're not sure who we would be on the other side. In the same way that we believe that without a strict diet we would hunker on our couches, uncontrollably eating pizza and ice cream, we also believe (without knowing we believe) that we need shame and judgment to keep us in line. Freeing ourselves means seeing that we are more than the sum total of our accomplishments, our relationships, our so-called failures, our body mass index and weight.

Being free takes first realizing we're in prison, and then questioning what imprisons us.

Peace takes naming what keeps us unruffled.

Joy takes realizing what separates us from it and challenging our familiar stories. And then giving up the wet, moldy baby blanket of identity we've been carrying around for our entire lives.

It's a process, not a onetime event; you've got to want your life back more than you want anything. You've got to have a glimpse, a taste that you aren't who you thought you were, and then you've got to want freedom so badly that you'll do whatever it takes. Which is to question each time you start comparing or blaming yourself or anyone else (because the aunt in the attic works both ways; it can either turn on you or on someone who happens to be standing by).

Is it true that I am lazy? What's the proof?

*   *   *

It's a process, not a onetime event;
you've got to want your life back more
than you want anything. You've got to have
a glimpse, a taste that you aren't who you
thought you were, and then you've got to want
freedom so badly that you'll do
whatever it takes.

Is it true that learning tai chi will save me from a horrible death by cancer I have not been, and may never be, diagnosed with? What's the proof? (Michael knew tai chi, but it didn't save him from prostate cancer.)

Is it true that my life is a mess because I gained ten pounds?

Was my life better before I gained the weight or were my thighs just thinner?

If thin or rich or famous people really have better lives, why are they always in rehab, getting divorced, or killing themselves?

Am I really the most screwed-up person on the earth? Really?

A wild joy follows when you realize you've been caught and are now free, when you fling open the prison door, walk outside, and gulp air and light for the first time in hours or days or weeks. Then you realize that instead of being either the bully or the child, you are the one who notices both. You sense who you were and what you knew before you defined things as good or bad, fat or thin, right or wrong. Before you became what you needed to be to be loved, you knew the holiness of trees and water and rocks. You knew the adults were a bit mad, but you loved them anyway. You had no doubt, not one, about who you were; you had wings, and now, you have them again.

In my fevered state,
I saw myself as old, cantankerous,
swaddled in Depends, and still bitter about
the now-dead people who hurt me fifty
years before, even if I couldn't
remember their names.

CHAPTER ELEVEN

The Four-Month Virus

When I called my doctor, two weeks after he told me that I would feel "right as rain," to say I was still sick, he replied, "I think you might have the four-month virus."

I had already spent six weeks splayed on the couch in my Cat's Pajamas nightgown with dirty hair, a hot-water bottle, and uncontrollable shivering followed by high fevers. I'd watched my entire list of take-me-out-of-my-misery movies: *Love Actually*, *The Devil Wears Prada*,

The Blind Side, Something's Gotta Give, Sleepless in Seattle, Notting Hill, Lord of the Rings: The Return of the King, and *Groundhog Day.* I'd listened to *Middlemarch* twice on my iPod, and fallen in love with Matt Bomer after watching five seasons of *White Collar.* The fact that he was gay, married with three children, and young enough to be my son did not mar my devotion. And although I could watch him and his swaying hips forever, I was done with being sick.

"I can't do this for another two and a half months!" I sputtered. "I have classes to teach, a book to write, and three trips that I've already bought airline tickets for! You told me I'd be better by now." I felt like a five-year-old on the verge of a tantrum.

"I thought you had the three-week-or-so virus," he said, "but apparently, you don't. And this four-month version is really going around; I've had quite a few patients with it. Since there's no bacterial infection in your blood, antibiotics are not going to help, so you're just going to have to see this one out."

When I put the phone down, I went into my familiar "This can't be happening" routine, followed by my usual "It could be worse" rationale: "Your house isn't getting bombed, you're not a sex slave or living in Iraq, you don't have Ebola, and water still comes out of the faucet.

So you have to stay on your couch for two more months. It's not the end of the world." Nothing helped. I was tired of being in my own skin and I wanted out.

In situations like these I give myself five minutes to "have a moan," as a friend says. I complain if someone will listen. I make a mental list of all the ways it isn't fair, how everyone else is meeting their best friends for lunch in cheerful restaurants with potted red geraniums and real white linen napkins while I am home, cough- ing in a flannel nightgown. I resent them all for being healthy and bright-eyed. And I resent them for not call- ing me hourly, bringing soup made with pastured bone broth, and asking what form of massage I'd like to have next.

On that particular day, I realized I was either going to spend the next few months in abject suffering because I didn't want what was happening to be happening or I was going to find a way to live as if I'd chosen it. I recalled a story that I'd read in a Byron Katie book when she visited someone with cancer in the hospital who was crying about her swollen body. The woman lifted the covers and showed Katie that one of her legs was twice the size of her other leg. "Oh," Katie said, "I see what the problem is: you think both your legs should be the same size."

Then I remembered working with Katie on my outrage when my father was dying and his wife wouldn't take him to chemotherapy, or remove the area rugs on which he tripped because of his shakiness from Parkinson's disease, or give him his medicine. After a few initial questions, Katie asked me for proof that my stepmother should be acting the way I wanted her to.

"That's what a wife does," I answered.

"But not your father's wife," she said. "And isn't the proof that it shouldn't be happening the way you believe it should that it's not?"

"Possibly," I said. I didn't like the direction this was going.

Her next question was who I would be and how I would feel without the belief that my stepmother should be different than she was. I was so surprised by the question that it was impossible to fall back on my well-oiled indignation, so without thinking I said, "Sad that my father is dying, and no longer at war with his wife. Peaceful, somehow."

"Yes, sweetheart," she answered. "It's your thoughts about your stepmother that are causing you suffering, not your stepmother herself. You are responsible for your own suffering, but only a hundred percent of it."

In her answer I could sense the sudden freedom of "a

sky powdered with stars" (as Milton wrote), and the possibility that I didn't need other people to change before I could be content. On the other hand—and there is always another hand—it meant pulling in the tentacles of blame, which was a radical reversal of my lifelong conviction that other people were misguided, but with a little more direction from me, they could be trained.

Just in case Katie was wrong about my thoughts being the cause of my suffering, I spent sixteen years after my father died testing out her theory by continuing to blame other people while appearing as if I was taking responsibility for my thoughts, feelings, and actions. The result was that I had a list of people with whom I had grievances, and toward whom I felt righteous indignation. But the news of the four-month affliction left me smack in the middle of my mind and its web of negative thoughts without the usual distractions of work and wasting time on the internet. I was so listless that I didn't care about work, the misdeeds of the oligarchy running the country, or the newest celebrity with botched face work.

Without my escapes, I started being acutely aware that living inside my mind was not a pleasant experience: on the same day, in the same two-hour stretch, with nothing happening but a cough, a fever, and my familiar negative thoughts, I could feel puffed up and resentful, or hurt and enraged at the people who had wronged me years before. In my fevered state, I saw myself as old, cantankerous, swaddled in Depends, and still bitter about the now-dead people who hurt me fifty years before, even if I couldn't remember their names. Since I knew that someday, even if it was during the last, possibly immobile month of my life, I would be alone with my thoughts, I decided to make friends with my mind by questioning my unwavering belief in my thoughts and opinions.

*　　*　　*

*Questioning long-held beliefs
about other people, reality, what was
and wasn't possible, freed me from seeing
myself as a child in a hostile universe with
big bad people doing big bad horrible
things over which I had no control.*

I began by making a list of everyone in my "doghouse," as my husband called it. (I needed two pages.) I wrote down what they did to me, what I thought they should have done, and how I felt about them.

The first person on my list was my colleague Larry,

who had lied to me and broken our contract together. Every time I thought of him, or worse, saw him at the grocery store by the avocados, I'd remember what he did and hate him more. I now focused on his face and our interactions. I asked myself whether it was true that he should have acted differently (answer: yes, yes, and yes), followed by the question about whether it was absolutely true that he should have acted differently (reluctant answer: no, because he did what he did). Then, I asked myself how I interpreted what he did (answer: that he had no regard for me, that our many years of working together meant nothing to him, that he was an immoral, corrupt, evil human being).

Even as I wrote that last part down, I knew my interpretations were lies. When I put my feelings of betrayal and anger aside, I knew that our years together were valuable to him, and that they had catalyzed his new career. And I remembered the well of support, love, and encouragement he'd given me. That he'd spent hours with me constructing an outline for a talk, which had then turned into the initial structure for one of my books.

Then I asked myself whom I was hurting by "shutting him out of my heart," as Buddhist teacher Stephen Levine called it. I also questioned whether I had any part in his actions. This last query was the sticky place because when I was fierce about telling the truth, I could no longer see myself as a victim. I had to acknowledge that I also had lied (by omission) to Larry. I saw that he was unhappy and didn't ask him why. I knew that he wanted to work for himself, not me, and didn't say that out loud. Then I thought about the people, even if it was twenty years ago, with whom I had broken agreements and acted selfishly. I realized I was capable of doing (and had already done to others) everything of which I accused him.

It took two and a half weeks of going through the doghouse before I started the process with my mother, and quickly, albeit reluctantly, I saw that I'd been wrong about her (as I always was in this part of the inquiry, with anyone, everyone). That she loved me as much as she could love me, that she did the best she could, given her circumstances, and that, as my friend Kim reminded me, although my mother had pulled me across the floor by my hair once, I'd dragged myself across the floor hundreds if not thousands of times by replaying that memory for fifty-five years.

When I saw my own part in the drama with my mother (or anyone), I no longer felt like a victim. It wasn't that I condoned what she or anyone else did—

the abuse, broken contracts, or lies. But questioning my thoughts and the feelings they produced (which amounted to questioning long-held beliefs about other people, reality, what was and wasn't possible) freed me from seeing myself as a child in a hostile universe with big bad people doing big bad horrible things over which I had no control.

As the weeks in viral confinement turned into months, I kept reminding myself that it was my thinking, not the situation, which was causing so much flailing. That there was nothing wrong. It took being vigilant with myself, refusing to get hysterical about how long it was taking to feel better, to stop the flailing. The more I stopped fighting the battles I'd already lost—having a sick body, arguing with events that had happened years before— the calmer I became. The lighter I felt.

By the eighth week of the virus, I started to feel inexplicably, unbelievably joyful. Living as if I'd chosen this respite, along with no longer being racked by late-night Black Dog thoughts (as Winston Churchill famously referred to his moments of depression), started to feel like a wish I'd granted myself behind my own back, since I knew that I would never have chosen to spend months at home without being ill. I was now savoring the fact that I didn't have to get in my car, or push myself to accomplish ten more things than there was time for in any given day. My new exercise routine—five-minute walkabouts in the garden (instead of my usual hour-long mountain hikes)—was slow enough to notice every step, every scent, every bird trill.

*   *   *

The more I stopped fighting the battles I'd already lost—having a sick body, arguing with events that had happened years before— the calmer I became. The lighter I felt.

By the ninth week of the virus, I felt as if I was treading on holy ground, as if I'd been given 3-D glasses and could see that what I'd previously experienced as a lackluster world was suffused with joy and tenderness, not for a particular person per se, but for this messy magnificent life. For the suffering we unknowingly cause ourselves and other people, and for the eternity of love waiting with quiet affection beneath it.

I couldn't quite figure out the purpose of being alive if I stopped working so hard to get more of what I already had.

CHAPTER TWELVE

Hummingbirds on My Fingers

For many years, I lived in a twilight zone between wanting more and having enough. Between knowing that having more (experiences, love, success) would not add anything to my life, and still believing that the point of life was the getting-of-more. Also, there was the letdown of not knowing what else to do; I couldn't quite figure out the purpose of being alive if I stopped working so hard to get more of what I already had.

For fifty-five years my father left the house at five in

the morning, worked all day, and walked in again at midnight. In his seventy-six years on earth he had four wives, two children, five hundred neckties, fifteen Mont Blanc pens, one hundred watches, and three dozen Paul Stuart suits. When he was diagnosed with lymphoma and could no longer work, he turned into fog. He had nothing to say—literally, nothing—and when you looked into his face, it was blank. I never knew it was possible to fall away like that. Without the ability to work hard and get more stuff with the money he made by working hard, he became utterly unmoored. Which is—unmoored, that is—how I felt six years ago when, after a series of protracted illnesses, my doctor told me it was imperative that I "rest more and work less. But only if you want to be alive in a year."

In desperation, I looked around for role models besides my father. Ann Patchett, a writer whose work I admired, wrote that if you weren't working on a book (which I wasn't), an hour of writing a day allows you to stay nimble with words. So I wrote every day. Sometimes a sentence came and I felt as if I was soaring on the lilt of a particular word. Purpling. Dauntless. Spangled. But most of the time I sat at my desk and plodded, wrote crummy sentences, flimsy paragraphs.

Then came the challenging part: I stepped outside

to see if the double ruffle peonies that one of my students gave me were growing. I gazed at the feathery new leaves of the Japanese maple trees. I looked up at the sky. I listened to the birds. But all the while, I felt as if I was going to get in trouble, as if I wasn't supposed to be looking at flowers or watching birds or smelling the air. It's two o'clock in the afternoon for God's sake, I'd say to myself, and there are girls getting raped in Africa, children starving in Syria, elephants being killed for their tusks. If you're not at your desk working, at least save a child or a whale or an ocean.

I know a therapist who only works two weeks a month. When she told me that, my first response was "You're not allowed to do that. It's against the rules. If you're privileged enough to have enough money to work two weeks a month, then you need to spend those two extra weeks saving the planet or, at the very least, the dogs that people throw off bridges." After I spoke, she looked inquisitively at me, as therapists are wont to do. "Whose voice is that?" she asked.

It's not a voice, I told her. It's the truth. Get to work.

A student recently told me that if she accepted the fact that losing weight by dieting didn't touch the root of her self-hatred, she was certain that she'd spend the rest of her life "on the couch with dirty hair in ever-expanding muumuus eating cream puffs and watching reruns of *The West Wing*."

Although dieting didn't solve what prompted it, at least "I'm doing *something*. Dieting is the constant in my life. It keeps the hope alive that whatever despair lies hidden will be resolved with weight loss. Even though I've been on dozens of ultimately failed diets, there's always a chance that the next one will be *the* one."

One of my wise teachers, Jeanne, pointed out that if I was working so hard that my health was suffering, I must have an unspoken belief that its potential benefits outweighed its costs—and that I would get something I didn't already have. Something upon which my life depended. Do you know what that is, she asked?

Jeanne was waiting for a reply. I tried to change the subject, since, like my students, I didn't want to know what I knew. Striving for some big thing in the future was the glue that kept the machine of my life together; without it, I was afraid I'd become a banana slug, oozing in contentment but going nowhere. Or like my father, who without that striving turned into fog.

"So," Jeanne said, "what is so important that having it is worth ruining your health?"

"Undeniable value and self-worth," I finally answered.

"And is it working?" she asked.

"Not so well," I answered. "When I am lonely or sick, I can't go to sleep clutching a bestseller list. And as I pad through the days, the familiar melancholy hasn't disappeared by having thinner thighs, knowing Matt, or reminding myself that people I don't know and will never meet like my book."

"What about just allowing the part that doesn't feel value or self-worth? Maybe it's not as bad as you think it is. Maybe it's just a feeling . . ."

Since feeling into and allowing what's here to be here is my practice, I do it (often while kicking and screaming on the way). And of course, in the end—and that day—it reveals itself as only a feeling, and like any other feeling, it most wants to be welcomed and witnessed as part of the pantheon of the thousand other feelings that have come and gone.

A few months after that session, I spent a few days filming a conversation with Eckhart Tolle. Within five minutes of being with him, it was clear to me that if he ended up on the park bench where he'd spent two years penniless, not one iota of his experience of worth or spaciousness would change. Not because he said so, but because with every step, with every word, he transmits quiet and infinite affection.

I've practiced meditating with a long line of teachers since I lived in India in my mid-twenties, but either because I wasn't ready to change or the language they were speaking didn't make sense to me, the nub of who I took myself to be (worthless, lost, unlovable) never shifted. And after meeting Eckhart, I saw that it never would. The chubby eleven-year-old with the crooked bangs was never going to feel lithe and lovely. But so what? Those self-images were frozen in time, and if I didn't invest them with meaning or take myself to be them, they could float through my mind without leaving a trace. In the years following my meeting Eckhart, it became apparent to me that it wasn't the thoughts about worthlessness that were the problem, it was that I took myself to be them. The very second I allowed the worthlessness to be there without engaging or reacting to it, I was free.

When I wrote my first book proposal, my father said, "Forget getting published, will you? Someone sent a Charles Dickens book to a publisher without attributing the book to Dickens, and it was rejected. What makes you think you're better than Dickens?" But then I remembered my writing teacher, Ellen Bass, and the fact that she'd published a book after receiving 154 rejections that she'd used as bathroom wallpaper. She was the living model for me, the proof that an ordinary human being with persistence and respect for the craft could be a writer. And since I'd always wanted to write, I decided that if it was possible for Ellen, it was possible for me.

*   *   *

> *Your life is nothing more than the hundred million moments, mostly ordinary, of padding to the kitchen and getting a cup of tea and cooking oatmeal for your kids and sitting in traffic or at your computer. It all comes down to one breath and then another, one step and then the next.*

When I met Eckhart and he said, "You find peace not by rearranging the circumstances in your life, but by realizing who you are at the deepest level," I knew in a flash that I wanted that more than I'd wanted anything, ever—and that that longing was at the bottom of every other want I'd ever had. Because without that, I'd always want more. But with that, I'd have what I was secretly convinced working obsessively or another person's love was going to give me: spaciousness, ease, and joy. I'd have everything.

I also knew that if Eckhart could know himself on the deepest level, I could, too. And that I had a choice. I could continue to pursue success and be like the actress in a *New York Times* article about Oscar winners, who described "swanning into the Academy Awards in a lavish gown provided free from a name designer on a Sunday, only to wake up in a Studio City apartment a week later with dead bouquets and no flashing light on the answering machine." Or I could place my attention on the want of all wants.

Finally I understood that if I truly longed for peace and lightness, clarity and joy, I didn't have to wait; I could have them now. If I wanted to feel like I was allowed to take up space here on earth, I could occupy the space I already had. And if I wanted to know who I was at the deepest level, I could keep bringing my attention back to the blaze of the life force before my attention constellated around a thought or a story.

The writer Annie Dillard said that "the way you spend your days is the way you spend your life." That your life is nothing more than the hundred million moments, mostly ordinary, of padding to the kitchen and getting a cup of tea and cooking oatmeal for your kids and sitting in traffic or at your computer. It all comes down to one breath and then another, one step and then the next. And when you get to the end of your life, it no longer matters whether you were once president of something (a company, a country), or whether you were on the *New York Times* bestseller list for fifty weeks or the recipient of a Nobel Prize. All that will matter is whether you flowered here in earth school. Whether you brought yourself to your relationships with kindness, or with reactivity. Whether you shut your heart or opened it, even in the face of rejection. Whether you know who and what you are beyond the thoughts that come and go, beyond the achievements that our gotta-get-more culture worships.

Now I write for five or six hours a day, and then I stand outside with my arms outstretched like tree limbs. Hummingbirds have become my constant companions. It took weeks of standing still as a statue for the first one to come close. They arrive in droves and I am often so dazzled by their iridescent beauty and feathery feet that I feel as if I am going to faint.

> *I realized I could keep living*
> *like a five-foot-tall piece of Velcro*
> *with giant pieces of past anxiety or*
> *anticipated future stuck to me—*
> *or I could stop.*

CHAPTER THIRTEEN

Crushed Stars

Last night I dreamt that my body was made of crushed stars and black space—and so was everything I saw or touched. Since I used to dream that a serial killer was loose in our house, waking up in a body of stars in a room of stars was a new occurrence. This morning when I opened my eyes I felt like air and light were looking through me, as if I'd gone to sleep as a person and woken up as a galaxy.

After thirty minutes I wasn't sure what to do. How

do stars get out of bed? How do they walk to the bathroom? Do stars eat eggs and toast for breakfast? Do they kiss anyone, or do they just glow? (Reality check: A few years ago, I discovered that stars are mostly made of hydrogen and, therefore, are very hot and extremely noisy. Also, that they are not shaped like stars. But oh well.)

That's when my mind began its centrifugal whirl and began picking up leftover feelings and self-images from the day before: how hurt I was at what Carolyn said to me; how special I felt after being asked to give a talk at a large venue. With each remembered circumstance, I added more layers of my grumpy, grandiose self. By the time I swung my feet over the side of the bed, I knew exactly who I was. I was needy and wounded. I was special. I was sad. I was a failure. I was a success. But I was definitely not a crushed star.

In my twenties, after I'd made love with a married man in my mother's cedar closet on top of my grandmother's mink coat, and left for India a short time later, where I lived like a nun for four months, I felt like two people. One longed to live in a cave and give up everything she had in order to discover the meaning of it all;

the other liked trouble and chocolate, and wanted, as Ouiser Boudreaux says in *Steel Magnolias*, more money than God.

Although I've moved on from wanting riches or caves, I still take myself to be an astonishing array of selves— and they change all the time. The way I saw myself when I was ten (moon face, bad hair, chubby legs, not popular with the boys) was different than at eighteen (long, straight, sought-after hair, suddenly popular with the boys, still chubby), which was different than at thirty (aspiring writer, bad hair again, emerging from years of obsession). None of it, or them, endures.

As I sat on the edge of the bed, I realized that I could keep this up for the rest of my life: every morning, when I open my eyes (and after that, throughout the day), I can keep slipping into my old, familiar selves the way I slip into my favorite clothes, layer by layer: my favorite day-of-the-week underwear, my lacy bra, my gray-striped cashmere socks, faded jeans, and pink cashmere sweater. I put on some hair product (enough, it must be noted, to make my hair stand up and walk off without me), my geeky-chic tortoiseshell glasses, and within a few minutes I'm recognizable as me again.

On that star-studded morning, I saw that, depending on the situations I've encountered the day before, I get dressed in my favorite beliefs, my well-worn feelings. By the time I brush my teeth, I am someone who either has enough or who is lacking. As I walk to the kitchen for breakfast, I walk as someone who is incredibly special or irreversibly doomed.

Drama becomes me. Enthralls me. But that morning I couldn't ignore how clunky I felt when dressed in it. How burdened. And I realized I could keep living like a five-foot-tall piece of Velcro with giant pieces of past anxiety or anticipated future stuck to me—or I could stop. I could choose to be a crushed star or I could choose to pledge allegiance to my history, my stories, my ideas of what should and shouldn't have happened.

I hate it when someone tells me I have a choice about having or feeling clarity or joy or lightness (even when that someone is myself); it feels like being told to cheer up, that the world is a happy place when I know it's falling apart. I'm used to blaming people, and then complaining about what a bad hand I was dealt. Getting dressed in layers of feelings and fears, while being burdensome, has the benefit of history, heft, and substance, whereas, let's face it, being a crushed star sounds pretty but isn't very practical when it comes to making tea or winning an argument.

But I may—don't hold me to it—be tired of getting dressed in my same old pink cashmere abuse; this daily re-upping process is beginning to feel exhausting. It reminds me of what my Buddhist teacher Lama Seden told me: even if you decorate your cell with sunflowers and roses, even if you put chintz and handmade lace on the bars, it's still a prison. Why not turn the lock, open the door, and walk out?

*   *   *

But each time I take the proverbial leap from the racket of my mind, there is a sudden, radiant freedom.

There isn't anything I want more—not love, not success, not even the new cool belt I saw online—than to walk out of the prison of this endless siren song of myself. When I walk in the forest, I want to notice the light through the trees instead of coming up with the brilliant thing I should have said to my friend last week. When I eat breakfast, I want to taste the toast and not the leftover hurt. The ongoing low-level discourse about why what happened shouldn't have happened—whether it be about stubbing my toe, what my husband or the president of the United States said, or how JoJo treated me yesterday—has not exactly led to clarity or ease.

I used to say in my retreats that attention is the way

you bless yourself with love. The moment of choosing to drag my attention away from the drama (and promise) of the story is the blessing-with-love part. Which means it feels like taking a flying leap into the unknown. (Last spring, as I held my breath, the baby finch in the nest outside the back door tried her first flight; she hopped to the edge of the beam and jumped. One second later, she was drowning in the swimming pool and I was soaking wet from saving her. Not exactly a poster child for jumping into the unknown.) But each time I take the proverbial leap from the racket of my mind, there is a sudden, radiant freedom, as if who I was taking myself to be a moment before has suddenly dissolved, and in its place is the incandescent shine and fierce white heat of a crushed star.

> *"No" and "I don't want to"*
> *are complete sentences. Also,*
> *being nice is overrated.*

CHAPTER FOURTEEN

What Remains

A few years ago my therapist of ten years said, "I think you're done, Geneen. You've worked hard, and you can continue, but I think you're done."

Done? While I knew that I might be finished with therapy someday, I didn't think done would look like this.

I thought I would be fixed. That all I needed was to try hard, do what I was told, feel what I'd never allowed myself to feel as a child, and my nervous system would be calm and cushioned; I'd live in parasympathetic mode like my husband does, where everything is already and always okay. Someone used your name, address, and social security number to buy a phone and charge a hundred dollars' worth of calls in one day? No problem, sweetheart: call Verizon, cancel the charges, and relax.

It's not that I imagined waking up as a completely different person; it's just that at the end of therapy, I thought my familiar obsessions and neuroses would have been scoured with quintessential Borax so only the sparkling, sane parts would remain. With the right combination of brilliant therapists and awakened spiritual teachers I'd be healed, permanently fixed, and for the rest of my life I'd be free.

Instead, there are times when I still feel like an exposed nerve. There are still situations—after a few sleepless nights, a long illness, or a series of frustrating interactions—in which I devolve into a state of bitterness and envy. And some mornings still find me repeating the mantra that Joseph Goldstein, my first Buddhist teacher, once uttered: "Oy vey, another day. Didn't we just have one yesterday?"

Being in therapy certainly had its bright moments. Sometimes it was like having a dream mother, like being transported from frozen tundra to a balmy tropical island. Sometimes when I was working with the trauma of physical and sexual abuse, it was horribly painful. It was also lifesaving and mostly effective (except for the therapist who charged me when I went on vacation because she said she was sitting in her chair and thinking about me). In therapy I learned that "no" and "I don't want to" are complete sentences, that being nice is over-rated, and that no feeling is intolerable. I learned that when I feel hurt or angry, it's always because one of my top three tunes is playing in the background of my mind: I'm a victim, I'm unworthy, and there's never enough.

I thought therapy would delete those songs. It hasn't. Every time an old part is triggered (which, admittedly, happens less often), it feels exactly the same as it has for years. When, for instance, the "I'm unworthy" part comes up, I am instantly a despondent three-year-old with an unavailable platinum-blond mother who is walking out the door. And when the bitterness-envy part is triggered, I act like a firecracker rolled in porcupine quills: demanding, loud, dangerous. Not someone you would invite to a dinner party.

The most surprising part of being done with therapy is that there is no one to whom I can hand my selves and say, "Here, you do it. You fix her/them. I'm not up to the task."

Like an infant waits in her crib, like a toddler waits to be picked up, like a twelve-year-old waits in an empty house for someone, anyone to come home, I never stopped waiting for someone to come and get me. I knew how to go through the motions of being a good client or a good spiritual student, but I secretly resented having to save myself. I believed, albeit unconsciously, that I'd already paid enough in sorrow and was now owed salvation by someone else.

*　　*　　*

At some point (it looks like this is it), therapy meets spirituality and fixing ourselves meets the realization that there is nothing more to fix.

For forty years there was always the next person, the next hope. A future in which I could dream myself whole without taking full responsibility for that wholeness, in the same way that many of us pin our hopes on the next diet, and the next after that.

"When," I sometimes ask my students, "does it become nonnegotiable to stop turning to food when you are not hungry?"

"When," I ask myself, "does it become nonnegotiable to refuse to swoon to my top three siren songs?"

It's the same question in different forms. As long as we keep hoping that someone is coming, we keep waiting. As long as we believe the answer is out there, we don't have to turn around and discover it now.

Every good-enough mother teaches her child that no matter how bad it seems—no matter how many rejections or scraped knees or broken bones there are—it is going to be okay. Maybe not the way we wanted or hoped it would be, but still okay. A good parent returns a child to the place where she can trust that although she might be bitter or hateful for a moment, it's not the end of the world. There is love here. There is light and quiet here. There is peace.

At some point (it looks like this is it), therapy meets spirituality and fixing ourselves meets the realization that there is nothing more to fix. There are always going to be challenges in this dimension of body-personality: plane flights will be missed, people will reject me, and whatever thrilled me last year will disappoint me this year. Just when I think I've got it all together, an earthquake occurs. Someone dies. I get ill. When I take myself to be the sum of what happened to me as a child or is happening at this very moment, I can never get it right for very long. When I take myself to be the unending always-forgiving space in which the drama is unfolding, I am already always fine.

Finally we have to fall on the sword of knowing what we know and stop pretending that we don't know it. Until that moment—and I seem to be a slow learner because it took decades of therapy and spiritual practice to get me here—we act like children who are stuck on the wrong planet, in the wrong bodies, with the wrong families, and we spend our time searching for more, better, loving parents and ever more creative/addictive ways out. And when we forget, we can gently remind ourselves that even that from which we want to be saved most of all—death itself—is just closing our eyes.

PART THREE

Into the Sublime

*I began to understand that
the question wasn't what I did,
it was how. And it wasn't about adding
more big experiences . . . it was about
showing up day to day.*

CHAPTER FIFTEEN

A Big Quiet

When Eckhart Tolle invited me to film a conversation with him for his television series, I was honored but didn't want to go. The filming was scheduled for December in Vancouver. Rainy, cold, snowy-when-it-isn't-rainy Vancouver. I'd read *The Power of Now* in 1999 when it was first published and liked it enough to buy a copy for a friend (who gave it back to me because she didn't understand it, or him, or why anyone would want to). And I'd been to a workshop with Eckhart at Esalen in 2000; it was in a crowded outdoor tent, and the friends with whom I went, the ones who would soon file for divorce, bickered incessantly.

Of seeing Eckhart Tolle for the first time, I only remember brief flashes: the numinous light reflected from the walls of the tent on the odd-looking man with big ears at the podium. The wave in his hair, his hard-to-place accent. I don't remember what he said, or how I felt about what he said. More memorable was that my friend, the wife of the bickering couple, got sick from the spicy garlic eggplant at Saturday's dinner and we left before the last session.

At the time of the phone call from Eckhart's office, more than a decade had elapsed since I'd attended that workshop, and Eckhart had become famous as a spiritual teacher. Still, I remembered his history. He'd been an anxious, depressed Cambridge-educated intellectual who, one night at the age of twenty-nine, reached a nadir of suffering, after which he had a shift (his words) into irrevocable peace and stillness. And, after rereading *The Power of Now*, I remembered what I was so taken with years before: the fact that he said, with absolute certainty, that it was possible to be in a human body and be truly at ease—and not because of anything you had, did, or looked like.

It's not that I hadn't had experiences of this ease; I'd lived at an ashram in India in the seventies, attended meditation retreats in the eighties, and had been part of an ongoing spiritual inquiry group for two decades. During the past thirty-six years, I'd spent weeks at a time feeling as if nothing was missing. Each time, the experience was like breathing in fresh oxygen after being trapped in an airless underground room for what seemed like centuries. Like popping out of a bad dream into a palace of starlight. But those glimpses were fleeting, even the ones that lasted a few months—and most of them were brought on by long retreats or catastrophes. Within a few post-retreat/disaster months, I'd return to ricocheting between bouts of self-doubt and wanting the next "more."

Since I'd been banging my head against the wall of discontent for a few decades, I figured it might be helpful to converse with someone who had already stopped. So, after deciding on the essentials—what I was going to wear (black dress, motorcycle boots)—I flew off to Vancouver.

From the outside, Eckhart looked like any other person, trending toward the unusual. His eyes were set far apart, he had a slight hump on his back, and he walked with a slow sway. He wore a teal blue sweater vest— not exactly fashion forward—that reminded me of my eighth-grade algebra teacher, Mr. De Lauria, with his bow ties and cable-knit vests. But it wasn't Eckhart's vest or walk or clear violet eyes that were remarkable; it was the feeling of being with a human sky. After hugging me, he regarded me with a combination of curiosity, warmth, and lack of pretense, as if to say, "So. Here you are," and the immediate effect it had on me was that I didn't feel awkward, or not enough, or dumb. I wasn't even aware of myself in the usual way. It was as if I'd been living inside a machine and had gotten so used to the drone of the engine that I'd forgotten that it was on. With him, only a big quiet remained.

One of the first things Eckhart asked me—after he mentioned he'd read my books and liked them very much—was what I was going to write about when I wasn't neurotic anymore. "When you are through writing about the trauma and abuse and addiction you've lived through, what then?" he asked. I wanted to say, "What makes you think there will come a time when I won't be neurotic or crazy?" I wanted to say, "One needs to suffer to create. What about Fitzgerald, Hemingway, and Van Gogh?" But the question so surprised me—no one had ever presupposed there would come a time when I wouldn't be neurotic—that all I could mumble was "Gee, I have no idea." Because, in fact, I didn't.

At dinner the first night, I watched his movements, listened to the cadence of his voice. He was deceptively ordinary and extraordinarily calm; he liked red wine, Nikes, and wind-up watches. But being with him was so challenging to what I called normal (i.e., being acquisitive, never having enough, defining myself by what I did) that it was like having dinner with someone from another star system. The waitress, a woman with bright red hair and a nose ring, asked me what I wanted. I answered that I'd like the broiled salmon with broccoli and a glass of Malbec wine, but what I really wanted to say, having just seen *When Harry Met Sally* for the umpteenth time, was that I wanted what Eckhart had. Then I decided, having only just met him, that even an oblique reference to orgasms might not be the best idea.

Since my early twenties I'd been haunted by the specter of getting to the end of my life without having fully lived, although I didn't know what that meant: traveling to far-flung and unspoiled places like Antarctica, the Amazon, the Galápagos? Adopting a foster child? Learning to skydive? But within a few months of meeting Eckhart, I began to understand that the question wasn't what I did, it was how. And it wasn't about adding more big experiences—I'd had plenty of those already (I didn't wash my right hand for two days after it shook Nelson Mandela's)—it was about showing up day to day. Was I actually present when I answered emails, planted strawberries, or listened to Matt tell me about his day, or was I careening around in my mind, fantasizing about the future, revisiting the past, wanting to get done with what I was doing so that I could get on to the next better thing? Since the answer was "anywhere but here," I decided to follow two of Eckhart's suggestions for thirty days. I figured that if careening was really better than showing up (i.e., breathing when I breathed, walking when I walked), I could easily go back to my old ways.

* * *

When your lifelong partner is concerned you have the flu if you stop complaining, it's a bit sobering.

My first practice was to stop complaining. When my office manager forgot to send out an email that invited people to an event I was teaching, I set up a different reminder system, but I didn't complain. When my bank account was hacked and I discovered someone was stealing money from it daily, I reported it to the bank and closed my account, but wouldn't allow myself to complain. When I found a mouse sitting next to me on the arm of my favorite chair, I screamed and ran out of the house, but did not complain. (Then, for anyone who may be interested, I walked back into the house, trapped it underneath an empty cottage cheese container, and brought it outside, screaming [is a scream a complaint?] the entire time.) But it wasn't just extreme situations; I stopped complaining to anyone about anything. I kept reminding myself of what I'd heard years ago: that complaining about what has already happened is like eating rat poison and waiting for the rat to die.

I soon realized—it took about ten minutes—that what I called conversations were, at least partially, a litany of complaints about who done me wrong, and an attempt to elicit outraged murmurs of agreement. Without shoring up the me that this shouldn't have happened to (but always, sigh sigh sigh, did), I wasn't sure what to talk about. (Could anyone actually *live* without complaining? Did Eckhart? I wanted to write and ask him, but that seemed like a backdoor complaint about how hard it was not to complain, so I decided against it.) Matt and I would get in the car, and I'd open my mouth to say, Can you believe what Oona did today?, but the words would catch in my throat like chicken bones and I'd ask about his day, or I'd open the window and look at the trees. Since I didn't tell Matt about my new resolve, and since I was unusually quiet, he kept asking me if I was ill. When your lifelong partner is concerned you have the flu if you stop complaining, it's a bit sobering.

My second practice was to be conscious of one entire breath, five or six times a day, for one minute. Since I was already breathing, it didn't seem like a stretch to put my attention on the beginning, middle, and end of a breath. To notice how it seemed to start in my belly, work its way up to my heart, throat, head, and back. After daily meditations in which I'd follow my breath for forty-five minutes, noticing five measly breaths a few times every day seemed like a cinch.

As the days passed, I noticed that I'd be walking in the forest, and instead of noticing the wild pale-yellow orchids I'd be thinking about dinner that night. I'd be walking to the kitchen, and instead of feeling the movement of one leg and then another I'd be thinking about the radiation from Fukushima, or whether the honeybees were going to become extinct, and if apples would still be around in ten years. It didn't take long before I realized why I was perpetually haunted by a fear of missing my life: I already was.

The very act of noticing how much I wanted to

complain, or how far into my thoughts I'd wandered, pierced the familiar trance I'd called "my life." I started noticing what I'd been missing: the first sip of tea, the barely perceptible lift of the wind on my face. Each time I refrained from complaining or noticed the full range of breath, I was startled by the vividness of what was in front of me, even if I'd seen it a thousand times before—a chandelier, a strawberry, my husband. "Be like a child," the Tibetan Buddhists say, "astonished at everything." For a few times a day every day, I felt like a child and understood for the billionth time that we become what we spend our time on: when I spend my time complaining, I find more and more to complain about and become an *alte kaker*, as they say in Yiddish (translation: a cantankerous old fart).

*   *   *

**I was startled by the vividness of
what was in front of me, even if I'd seen
it a thousand times before—a chandelier,
a strawberry, my husband.**

There are months now when I am definitely not my same old cantankerous self and everything seems to be made of a kind of fizzing light—arms, legs, banana slugs, garbage. On those days I feel like Dustin Hoffman in *Tootsie*, whose character has been impersonating a female soap opera star. He turns to his paramour, Jessica Lange, and says, "I was a better man with you as a woman than I ever was with a woman as a man." I am a better me as not-me than I ever was as me.

Then there are the other days. The slog days. I wake up grumpy and, within thirty seconds, enter the rat maze of my thoughts. It's almost as if the spaciousness has suddenly become unnerving, as if I've convinced myself that although I was dumb enough to drink the Kool-Aid of believing that freedom from suffering was possible, I'm over it now and can get back to the comfort of feeling grumpy, rejected, and worthless. (It reminds me of my students who, after spending seven blissful days on retreat in which food was not a problem, get home and are furious with me because they fell for the possibility that their whole lives could be like that.)

On those days I feel trapped in a familiar underground room, and it takes a while to return to life aboveground. But when I pop back into the stillness, it always feels the same: as if I've just been dreaming myself and am now awake. And each time, the sweetness and stillness of return feel more and more like home.

> *I learned a lot from*
> *spiritual practice—about ease*
> *and loveliness and my crazy mind—but*
> *it didn't dispel my fears of death.*

CHAPTER SIXTEEN

The Breaths I Have Left

When I was eight my father gave me a copy of *Death Be Not Proud*, a book by John Gunther about the life and death of his son Johnny, and by the time I turned the last page—and I say this in the kindest possible way—I'd become a bit of a hypochondriac and completely death-obsessed. Not only did I start worrying that every time I got a headache I had a brain tumor (as little Johnny did), but I also became convinced that the end was near. When my parents walked out the door,

I wondered whether I would see them again. When my brother went to Mike May Day Camp, I worried he would get run over by a car. I just couldn't believe that eight-year-old Johnny had died—and that everyone else would die as well. It didn't seem fair, it didn't seem right. Or, as Woody Allen said, when asked how he felt about death, "I am strongly against it."

In my twenties and thirties I elevated my death-obsession into a spiritual practice. I learned Buddhist meditation, went to graveyards with teachers who were intent on teaching us what I'd known for years: *Life is short. People die. You will be amongst them.* I traveled to India and saw the burning ghats in Benares. I witnessed how long it took a body, with all its bones and muscle, hair and eyes, to turn to ashes. (FYI: a long time. I had to get a Coke halfway through and come back for the rest.) I learned a lot from spiritual practice—about ease and loveliness and my crazy mind—but it didn't dispel my fears of death. If anything, it exacerbated them because I became more aware of the shortness of life. My life in particular.

There is an old saying in Buddhist circles that this human life is so precious that it is as if each one of us is like a turtle that lives in the ocean and comes up for air every hundred years. If by chance that rising turtle put its head through a bucket floating on the ocean's surface it would be extremely rare. Attaining a human life is even rarer than that. So, since you have a chance in this one precious life to discover who you really are—your true nature—don't waste a single second.

Talk about pressure.

As I headed into my forties and fifties, people around me were dying or had died. My father, my dear friend Lew, my cat. My aunt Bea. My friend Rosemary. And every time, it was the same: How could a person (even those with four legs) be here one day and gone the next? Death was so irreversible, so forever—unlike, say, buying a pair of shoes from Zappo's with a 365-day return policy.

But then something unexpected happened. During a routine medical procedure my throat closed, my heart rate skyrocketed, my blood pressure dropped, and I had the strange sensation of leaving my body. I was conscious enough to realize that this was the Big It: I was dying. I remember being surprised that it was happening so quickly, and on an ordinary day in September. (I was hoping for harps and orchids and long soulful glances of loved ones when I died, not a chilly, antiseptic examination room with a nurse with a purple happy face pinned on her smock and a doctor with a wandering eye who kept imploring me to look at him.)

Although there were many compelling insights during and after that near-death experience, one that has remained with me is the visceral understanding that all my years of being death-obsessed weren't actually about dying or death; they were about life. They weren't about fear of the end, they were about longing to be awake in the middle (also known as the present). I wanted, as the poet Mary Oliver says, to spend my life "married to amazement," not wedded to regret or exhaustion.

After the medical procedure I realized that this life wasn't a dress rehearsal for some bigger, better promise around the corner. This was it, and my breaths were numbered. I didn't know how many breaths I had left—an eighty-year-old person takes about 672,768,000 breaths in a lifetime, which meant I'd used up three quarters of my actuarially allotted breaths—but it became apparent that no matter how charming I was or how many organic pomegranates I ate, not dying was not an option.

★　　★　　★

Over and over, with each day and each choice, I asked myself: Is this something on which I want to spend the breaths I have left?

Within a few days of being home from the hospital, I made a list of what I loved. Of what I would have regretted not doing (more of) had I died in the examination room. The list was short: being with my husband, family, and friends; playing with my dog; being outside; writing and teaching. I began quitting things in which I didn't want to participate. I began saying no to parties I didn't want to go to, invitations I didn't want to accept. I quit a graduate program in which I was enrolled, and I started working on a book I'd wanted to write for years. I spent more time with trees, particularly a maple tree in our driveway. I told my husband regularly what I cherished about him and our life together. Over and over, with each day and each choice, I asked myself: Is this something on which I want to spend the breaths I have left?

Eight years have passed and I am still asking that question. Not always, of course. Sometimes when my husband and I are fighting, revenge supplants breaths in my mind. But even then I frequently pull myself back from the brink and remember that we are only alive for a brief run, and I don't want to miss a breath.

> *As I become curious*
> *(rather than reactive) about my*
> *catastrophic tilt, I see that at its core*
> *is a frightened ghost child living in*
> *a family in which each day felt*
> *like the end of days.*

CHAPTER SEVENTEEN

Waiting for the Apocalypse

Since childhood I've been enthralled by disaster scenarios and fantasies of what I would do and where I would go when things got too terrible to stay. I'm not sure if it was knowing that a few dozen relatives were killed in Auschwitz because they didn't leave Germany in time, or that living with my abjectly miserable-with-each-other parents unhinged my nervous system, but I lived in anticipation of the next cataclysmic shoe to drop. I ran away twice, once when

I was eight and got as far as the end of the block before my uncle Murray saw me, asked where I was going with my pink-flowered suitcase, and coaxed me back with the promise of Hostess cupcakes with white squiggles on top. (Even then, the lure of cupcakes trumped my best intentions.) The second time I ran away, I was six-teen and made it as far as a hotel in Manhattan—being a stowaway on a train wasn't my style—but since I was using my mother's credit card, I wasn't exactly hard to find. As I walked into the hotel room, my mother called and said, "Get home this *INSTANT!*" And that was that.

Regardless of any tilt toward catastrophe, however, the truth remains that on any ordinary day, multiple, unanticipated disasters are lurking: car and bicycle accidents, a sudden heart attack while on an airplane or treadmill, someone we know/love getting run over by a drunk driver. Add to that the danger of falling in the bathroom, hitting one's head and getting a brain injury—and it's a miracle that any of us get out of bed in the morning. Still, despite the incipient terrors of living in this vulnerable human body, most of us man-age rather well by engaging two highly effective defense mechanisms: denial and repression. We keep having babies, making plans for the future, living as if death only happens to other people. We push scary scenarios out of our minds.

Enter climate science.

My friend Lorraine reels off another climate-science fact every time we talk: a hundred kinds of plants and animals are going extinct every day; honeybee colonies are collapsing; shelves of Arctic glaciers are crashing into the ocean at a much faster rate than anyone ever imagined. Lorraine thinks that the people who are dying now of cancer, Parkinson's, and Alzheimer's are the lucky ones. "They are dying with people they love around them. The rest of us will be dying long, drawn-out, horrific climate-related deaths," she says.

Lorraine implores me to move to Australia, where she lives, because "at least no one will nuke Australia; it's not important enough. Also, the weather is beautiful and although climate change will also wreak its havoc here, you'll most likely have a few more months to live than if you stay in California."

"What about all those spiders and snakes and sharks?" I ask, reeling off what I know about Australia's poisonous creatures from a website I recently discovered: "Australia is home to the ten deadliest animals in the world. All of those animals want you dead. There is a reason Australia is surrounded by nothing but water. God is trying to protect you from the hell trapped within." Even Bill Bryson, one of my favorite authors, wrote about the fact that all of the most poisonous creatures on earth live in Australia, while also proclaiming that he loved the country itself.

*　　*　　*

When I acknowledge that there really is a chance that we may not have much longer on this earth, it forces me into unspeakable gratitude for being given this much time.

As susceptible as I am to disaster scenarios, I know that making decisions from fear is a terrible idea. I tell Lorraine the story of my friend Sally's next-door neighbor who moved to higher ground during the 1982 mudslides in Santa Cruz, and within twenty-four hours was dead from her safer house collapsing while the house from which she moved still stood. "Isn't it conceivable," I ask Lorraine, "that Matt and I could move to Australia for safety's sake and die within days from a poisonous snake bite?" "I suppose it is," she answers, "but at some point, you make a decision based on probabilities."

To educate myself about probabilities, I read Bill McKibben's *The End of Nature*, Naomi Klein's *This*

Changes Everything, David Suzuki's *The Sacred Balance*, as well as dozens of articles by concerned scientists, including one by Yale University scientist Wei Liu, who warns that the collapse of a vital Atlantic Ocean current would create an ice age for the Northern Hemisphere.

And while there are people—Naomi Klein is among them—who are still hopeful we can turn this ship around, the trajectory of history and corporate greed is not in the earth's favor. "We're in a giant car heading towards a brick wall and everyone is arguing where they're going to sit," says David Suzuki.

For years, I tried and failed miserably at being an activist, but the more marches and meetings I attended, the more enraged I became and the more my stance became one of us and them, which was the very same as that of the oil companies and polluters. Although I don't exactly know what actions to take now, I am certain that stoking hatred will make me bitter and even more obstreperous than I already am. I also know, from years of working with addiction, that being *against* what's apparently wrong is less effective than being *for* what isn't. But that doesn't cut the loop of the catastrophic thinking or the intense desire to repress it all by distracting myself with pretty things to see or wear or eat.

My friend Jeff says, "Every time the world around me

gets too dark, I think, 'Time to plan a trip to an excit-ing place!'" He's been to all seven continents and five oceans many times and is now about to visit the Amazon to swim with the pink dolphins. "Would you and Matt like to come?" he asks. The thought of swimming in the Amazon brings back memories of the multiple times I've contracted amoebic dysentery from doing exotic things like swimming in the Amazon, and I politely decline. But that leaves me alternately pretending that life as we know it has not changed, and convinced that since we will all be dead in ten years, I might as well drink tequila (before the agave plant becomes extinct) and eat chocolate (before the cacao bean vanishes).

And yet, I don't know anyone in my community who wants to discuss the end of days. I feel like a mad doomsday hysteric until I remember that according to Bart Ehrman, a religious scholar, Jesus was a doomsday prophet. This comforts me immensely, not only because that was more than two thousand years ago and we are still here, but also because if someone as illuminated as Jesus believed in the apocalypse, I figure I'm in good company.

Given that a nuclear bomb has not yet hit and there still seem to be at least a few more years of the emerald sweetness of life here on earth, the question becomes what to do now. Do I talk about climate science with my friends, despite their not wanting to hear? Do I walk around in a tempest of grief and anxiety? Distract myself with exotic trips like swimming with pink dolphins in the Amazon? Continue to sign petitions, give money to animal and earth causes? Is that enough? If this is truly the end of days, what would I do or say differently from what I am doing and saying now?

As I become curious (rather than reactive) about my catastrophic tilt, I see that at its core is a frightened ghost child living in a family in which each day felt like the end of days. Anticipating the next worst thing colored every breath, every interaction, every meal. As soon as I allow myself to name and feel the imprint of that conditioning, kindness emerges for the child, the parents, and the situation itself. And the madness unwinds, since I am no longer either identified with the hysteria or fighting against it.

There is awe here as well. For the mist drifting above the tree line outside my window. For the one brave rose left in my winter garden. For the water falling from the sky. When I acknowledge that there really is a chance that we may not have much longer on this earth, it forces me into unspeakable gratitude for being given this much time. Or any time at all. Fear and anxiety are replaced by grief for the damage we've wrought, and a resolve to do what I can to protect what remains.

Thirty years ago, I read a Ram Dass quote (that I have never been able to locate; this is a paraphrase): whether we are sailing into the New Age or heading toward Armageddon, our work is exactly the same: to quiet the drums of fear, speak from a soft heart, and act from our shared humanity.

Yes. Yes.

> *When we're convinced*
> *we have to earn joy, we don't notice*
> *the ten thousand places in which it is*
> *already waiting, asking, waving*
> *for our attention.*

CHAPTER EIGHTEEN

What Isn't Wrong

The rain in the South of France that summer was relentless; my feet were never dry, and because I had packed as if I was going to the Riviera instead of a monthlong retreat in a moldy brown tent at Thich Nhat Hanh's Plum Village Center, I didn't have a raincoat. Morning meditations at six a.m. were cold, wet, and clammy; evening meditations were waterlogged and frosty. Although I was supposed to be focusing on my breath or listening to a talk about the seven heaven realms, I was convinced I was trapped in a clammy Buddhist hellhole.

One sodden morning Thich Nhat Hanh changed topics from Buddhist sutras to toothaches. "How many of you don't have a toothache right now?" he asked.

I can't remember whether everyone raised their hands, but there was definitely a quorum of nontoothache candidates in the room.

Then he said, "When we have a toothache, all we can think about is going to the dentist or taking medication to stop the pain. But when we don't have a toothache, we don't appreciate the many benefits of the nontoothache state. So, please, turn to one of your brother or sister *sangha* members and take five minutes to appreciate the state of not-a-toothache."

And just like that, as I listed all the things that weren't wet and didn't hurt or ache, I noticed myself feeling light and undeniably happy. It was still raining and my feet were still damp, but my attention was no longer a constellation of what was wrong. Once again, I realized that it wasn't the dampness, it's never the dampness (and that doesn't mean I would choose to wear wet shoes or go back to Plum Village); dampness isn't miserable, it's just dampness. That's it. That's all.

At its most basic, meditation is about watching

thoughts without identifying with them (i.e., taking yourself to be them). You notice the mind activity
itself, and that you have a choice—you've always had
a choice—about where to direct your attention. You
can engage with the content of your thoughts (i.e., I
am going to get pneumonia if I stay wet like this for one
more second) or you can notice what isn't wrong (the
fact that you are breathing, a bird is chirping, you are
still aboveground). You can break the trance by using the
senses: seeing color, hearing the scrape of a pen across
the page, smelling the air when it rains. You can come
back to what you've always had, what's always been
here, and, in T. S. Eliot's words, ". . . know the place for
the first time."

*   *   *

*After so many years of so many practices
and so many prayers, I have only one left:
let me remember to pay attention to the
ordinary, not just to the extraordinary.*

My friend Kate, who has spent five years undergo-
ing one grueling chemotherapy treatment after another,
as well as their attendant exhaustion, hope, disappoint-
ment, and discomfort, and has decided to stop all treatment, said, "It's taken me so long to realize that just

being able to walk around TJ Maxx and buy a black tote with outside pockets makes me indescribably happy. I've been so pitched to the future, to when or if I get well, that I've missed so many walks, sounds, and totes. In the name of extending my life for five or ten years, I've missed the one I've had."

When we think a meaningful life is about grander things than being able to walk around TJ Maxx, we miss the joy of being able to walk at all. When we're convinced we have to *earn* joy, we don't notice the ten thousand places in which it is already waiting, asking, waving for our attention.

After so many years of so many practices and so many prayers, I have only one left: let me remember to pay attention to the ordinary, not just to the extraordinary. To finding the perfect tote with outside pockets and to the sound of my feet walking, click click click, as I do.

As I skulked to the bathroom, I decided that I really was hopeless, a spiritual failure. Then, as I was brushing my teeth, I thought, but in that case, why not be hopeless in a blue vest?

CHAPTER NINETEEN

The Blue Vest

We saw it in the window of a store on a side street in San Francisco: the piece of clothing for which I'd been waiting without knowing I'd been waiting. "Come and be enthralled," it whispered. "Let my fringes anoint you." I slipped into the floor-length vest like a swan would slip into her wings, and I glided around the room as if the store was my lake. As I passed the rows of jackets and racks of shoes, I felt like Harry

Potter in his invisibility cloak, except that mine was made of manifest blue enchantment.

"Do you like it?" I asked my husband when I emerged from the swoon. Although Matt's wardrobe consists mainly of rugby shirts, khaki pants, and New Balance shoes in various stages of wear, he has uncanny wisdom when it comes to women's sartorial plumage.

"Where might you wear this?" he asked, eyeing the shimmering blue fabric. "It doesn't seem appropriate to wear around the house or to Whole Foods . . ."

Oh yeah, I thought, that's right. We live in the country, down a mile-long gravel road where our daily companions are owls, oak trees, and deer. When I thought about flouncing around on gravel in a silky vest, it broke the spell; I felt like my student Gloria, who said that when she eats a piece of chocolate she feels like Cinderella becoming a princess, but when the chocolate is gone she feels like a pauper again. I told Scott, the salesperson (we were now on a first-name basis), that although I really did like the vest and was surprised my husband didn't have to don his sunglasses to tolerate its blinding beauty, I'd call in a few days to see if it was still there.

At dinner with friends that night the conversation was lively, but visions of blue distracted me: the way the vest pooled around my legs, changed colors, became indigo then cobalt then slate. Wearing it is like wearing the ocean, I thought, as I took a bite of Caesar salad. And although it's true, I can't wear it to plant radishes in the garden, I have to wear something to restaurants or lectures; why not this?

The next morning I decided to buy the vest. But as I started walking to the phone, the fight with myself began. I want to be the kind of person who is no longer enchanted by things. If I was born in Asia, I'd be a wise elder wearing plain blue cotton shirts and long gray braids. I'd be doing tai chi outside in town squares, playing checkers and consorting with other braided women about how best to handle the rabble-rousing young hellions. I need to meditate more, disengage from my thoughts—not buy more clothes. Because when I am on my deathbed —which is closer now than it was last year or the year before—having a blue vest won't matter— and I want to spend my energy on what does.

As I skulked to the bathroom, I decided that I really was hopeless, a spiritual failure. Then, as I was brushing my teeth, I thought, but in that case, why not be hopeless in a blue vest?

It shouldn't be a conundrum, but it is.

I shouldn't love things, but I do.

Although I am well aware that you become what you love, as the Sufis say, I don't seem to be able to help being who I am or loving what I love, especially beauty in its myriad forms. The dazzle of first morning light. My motorcycle boots with the red rhinestone boot belt. Matt's face. A blue vest. To the extent that there is a quandary, it is with my belief that beauty is defined by its forms, particularly those that are young and dewy-faced or silky and impractical.

As a teenager, after reading hundreds of *Glamour* magazines, I was convinced that the antidote to feeling ugly was to become an actress or a model (and be seen as being beautiful). In eighth grade I told my classmates I'd been cast as an orphan in the Broadway show *Oliver*, in which Bartley Larson, one of our friends, was already starring. Unfortunately, since the whole class was given season tickets to the show and I never appeared in it, they discovered that I had an elastic relationship with the truth.

In tenth grade I played the role of an ailing debutante in a skit opposite my real-life heartthrob Martin How-ard, and bombed so completely (I had a hard enough time being myself; being someone else was impossible) that in the auditorium of a few hundred people, only my mother clapped when I took my bow.

Undeterred in my attempts to mesmerize people, I decided to become a model. Wearing a white A-line dress with pale blue lines and looking like a well-outfitted tent, I renamed myself Geneen Howard, dragged my brother to the Barbizon School in Manhattan, and presented myself to the receptionist. She asked me to get on the scale (I weighed 110 pounds), told me I was too fat and that my legs were too short.

When it became obvious that a trend of five-foot-three stubby-legged models would not begin with me, I narrowed my focus to keeping my skin smooth, my muscles toned, and my hair shiny in hopes of approximating a culturally acceptable version of "attractive." It worked. Until it didn't. At thirty, I looked like I was in high school. At forty-five or fifty, I looked like I was thirty. But at sixty-five, I could walk down the street with my hair on fire, as my friend Catherine says, and no one would notice. Although I still feel youngish, and that "everyone my age is an adult, whereas I am merely in disguise," as Margaret Atwood puts it, I am still somewhat shocked when I ask for a senior discount at the movie theater and there is no protest. If I see a friend for the first time in a few years, I wonder whether he's had a stroke or is dying because he looks so diminished. And then I realize that he's probably wondering the same about me.

*   *   *

*If I see a friend for the first time in
a few years, I wonder whether he's had a stroke
or is dying because he looks so diminished. And
then I realize that he's probably wondering
the same about me.*

At first I was confused by getting older (why can't I read the small print?), then offended (for God's sake, who on earth could read this?), and finally, I surrendered (progressive lenses, I decided, were eye jewelry: cool). But just when I thought I'd reached an aging plateau, my chin disappeared into my neck and I started looking like my jowly father when he was dying. My arms soon followed. They began looking speckled, like I'd just taken off a polka-dot sweater (who even knew that arm cellulite existed?), and every morning there were more lines around my eyes and my mouth, although, because I couldn't see without my glasses, I wasn't certain.

Despite the fact that everyone who doesn't die young gets old, I must have believed that getting older was a choice, and since I wasn't making it, it wouldn't happen to me. And until recently (except for the eye jewelry), I haven't been a model of "aging with grace." Just as I used to stand in front of the mirror and pull back the fat on my thighs to see what they would look like if I lost twenty pounds, I pull back what Anne Lamott calls "the Utah desert on my neck" to see what I would look like without it. It's as if I fantasize that looking younger will give something back to me that I lost (besides my chin). Or that there's only one way to see the lines around my eyes or the folds above them: as traitors to be vanquished. Since I've ruled out plastic surgery for many reasons (death by anesthetic, threats of divorce, feeling as if my head is in a tourniquet post-face-lift), I am left with either fighting the ever-increasing effects of having lived this long or taking time out to reconsider the meaning of beauty.

Years ago my teacher Jeanne told me to think of my eyes as catchers' mitts. "See what is there," she said, "and allow yourself to take it in, be filled by what you see," which reminded me of what the novelist Albert Cossery wrote: "So much beauty . . . , so few eyes to see it." Could it be that beauty is about seeing, and not about being seen? And that though a particular form is the transport mechanism (the way that bread is the delivery system for butter), it is the effect of beauty— the rapture of it—that actually elevates and inspires. And while it's true that I had moments of rapture when I was acceptably attractive, I also had months of melan-

choly. My well-defined neck and butt were not caus-
ative in either the rapture or the melancholy. The only
thing—and I've traveled the earth looking—that has
brought me ever-present joy is to see what I see, wake
myself to the splendor in small things, and appreciate,
appreciate, appreciate.

★   ★   ★

Could it be that beauty is about seeing, and not about being seen?

Which brings me back to you-know-what.

"It is rather striking," Matt said, when I opened the
UPS package in which the blue vest was nested. "And
when you wear it, you can quote Liberace and say: 'I
didn't come here to go unnoticed.'" I reminded myself
that Matt has many fine qualities—humor, generosity,
a heart as wide as the Grand Canyon—and that in our
twenty-nine years together he has stopped me from
looking like a shrub and a bear, but that he's not always
right. Sometimes he misses the point of adornment for
the joy of it, which is, in my opinion, one of the splen-
dors of having a body. And since that body comes with
a multitude of challenges, it's important to revel in the
available joys.

The ancient philosopher Plotinus said, "Beauty must

ever induce a wonderment and a delicious trouble . . . a trembling that is all delight." Now, instead of pulling back the skin on my neck, I wear the blue ocean to buy zucchini at the store. I go to parties, and when everyone else is wearing T-shirts and jeans, I'm dressed in blue enchantment, awash in delight.

> *In the next moment
> the person I usually knew as myself
> wasn't there, but something else was.
> And it was huge and lush, utterly
> still and completely at ease.*

CHAPTER TWENTY

Not Minding What Happens

When I was in Ojai, California, last year, I visited the home of Krishnamurti, the philosopher who died in 1986. I sat in the room in which he ate, walked the land on which he walked, and meditated under his favorite tree. I was hoping I would see what he saw, feel what he felt, know what he knew. I was hoping for enlightenment-by-osmosis.

In *Krishnamurti's Notebook*, a book of his journal writings, he describes the delicacy of a rosebush planted in a container on a corner of a deck in Paris. I was struck by the fact that although he was in the city that housed Monet's *Water Lilies*, Rodin's sculpture garden, and chocolate croissants, Krishnamurti dared to attend to the smallest beauty. And that often when he did, "the otherness" would arise. And it was so huge, so encompassing, that it dissolved everything we usually think of as a person—thoughts, emotions, beliefs. He wasn't frightened of it. He didn't fight it. He didn't conjure up, say, his relationship with his mother so that he could become his familiar self and climb back into the shape of his personality as he knew it.

I've had glimpses of this otherness; one of them occurred yesterday, when I was sitting in my backyard. My mind was burbling on like an all-news radio station about my friend Mo, who was supposed to call me back and didn't, the fact that I needed to call the guys who pump out the septic tank because it's been too long, the emails that were piling up, and the dream I'd had the night before about meeting Patti Smith in front of a taco food truck. Then, in an effort that felt like chewing nails, I pulled my attention from the noise machine of my mind to the sun on my legs, the smell of sky, and the rustling of leaves in the wind. In the next moment the person I usually knew as myself wasn't there, but something else was. And it was huge and lush, utterly still and completely at ease. Thoughts were flying by in the background but since I wasn't involved with them, they disappeared without a trace.

Then I remembered the septic tank, and my usual sense of self—rushed, slightly irritated—sprang like a Slinky into its tightly coiled form. And with the onrush of thoughts, I noticed an almost imperceptible relief, like the feeling of being able to speak in English after I've spent a week in Mexico, reaching for the Spanish words for bathroom, bank, and bed. Home at last.

*   *   *

When you stop minding what isn't here (a friend, a house, a spouse), you can open yourself to what is.

Krishnamurti writes, "woke up in the middle of the night, with the otherness in the room. It was there with great intensity, not only filling the room and beyond but . . . deep down within the brain, so profoundly that it seemed to go through and beyond all thought, space and time. . . . Strangely every time this takes place, it's something totally new, unexpected and sudden . . . beyond all thought, desire and imagination. . . . It's not an illusion."

One night someone in an audience of a few hundred people asked Krishnamurti his secret, the essence of his teaching. Speaking in a soft voice, Krishnamurti's answer was "I don't mind what happens." So simple, I thought, but not easy. Although I have a visa to the country of Otherness, I don't live there. I keep returning to my familiar self like a toddler keeps running back to her mother.

I thought of our friend Clementine, who, a few hours after escaping from the fire that destroyed her home, arrived at our house. "Everything is gone," she said, "even my favorite pair of red Dansko shoes. Even my dark green leather motorcycle jacket, my new silk underwear. Even the bank that was holding my safety-deposit box with my jewelry and passport burned down." We cried about her house, the deer with the broken knee living under her deck, and the flock of quail she fed every day on her porch. "I don't think they made it to higher ground," she said, tearfully.

A few hours later, after drinking tea and wrapping ourselves in fuzzy blankets, I said, "It's probably true that everything is gone, but let's hold out for the possibility that your red Danskos are still there, on top of a heap of ashes."

During the first week after the fire, Clementine was careful about not allowing her mind to wander to what she had lost, or where she would live, or the fact that she didn't have insurance or savings enough to last long. She was awash in grief and gratitude for being alive, and for the generosity of people she knew and strangers in stores. (While shopping for socks in her favorite store, a stranger, upon hearing the story of the fire, bought Clementine a burgundy cashmere sweater, after which I told her that she should go shopping in Silicon Valley among the billionaires. Someone might buy you a house, I said, or a small island.)

Since she had nothing to lose, she had nothing to protect. It was like living with someone without skin, whose heart was cracked open, whose face was lit. "If I don't think about what I lost," she said, "nothing is missing."

It seems that when you stop minding what isn't here (a friend, a house, a spouse), you can open yourself to what is. And when you do, it feels as if you've popped out of a small, cramped costume you've been wearing for many lifetimes. The boots were too tight, the buttons had fallen off, and although you were reluctant to let them go—they were so familiar that they'd taken the shape of you—the otherness of freedom calls you, even when you've unzipped into something or someone you don't recognize. Even when what remains is only the toe of a ruby slipper on the heap of what you once called your life.

Look up.

CHAPTER TWENTY-ONE

Snorkeling in the Night Sky

*How should we be able to forget those ancient
myths about dragons that at the last minute turn into
princesses who are only waiting to see us once beautiful and
brave; perhaps everything terrible is in its deepest being
something helpless that wants help from us.*
—*Rilke*

Night comes swiftly like "a great, dark, soft thing,"
and for most of my life I've greeted it reluctantly,
as if behind the darkness lurked terror and shattered
hearts. My mother says, "You were a fast napper from
the day you were born. Other kids went down for two
hours. You slept for twenty minutes and were up for the
rest of the day." Even as an infant, I didn't want to sur-
render to that dark, soft thing.

187

After an early menopause I started waking up three, four, five times a night. At first I tried natural remedies (melatonin, bio-identical hormones, cortisol adaptogens), then unnatural ones (drugs). But since I have a paradoxical reaction to drugs—Ambien kept me awake, and during the second week I took Ativan (the first week was heavenly)—I developed suicidal proclivities and wanted to jump off a bridge. Then I downloaded sleep music, tried brain-balancing techniques, listened to books on tape (*Middlemarch*, *Team of Rivals*, and *A Passage to India* are still my favorites; also anything by Bill Bryson, except he makes me cackle, which wakes up my husband, which makes two of us wide awake at three a.m.). Still, night after night, my eyes flew open like clockwork—and with them began the rattling of my mind and the descent into the catastrophic (the pain in my chest is congestive heart failure, I'm sure of it), the ugly (I've been married to the wrong person for thirty years), and the uglier (was that noise a rapist? Where's my gun? Oh, right, I don't have one).

In her book *Marrow*, Elizabeth Lesser calls this litany "middle of the nightism," and she urges us not to believe any thoughts that occur between midnight and six in the morning. To that wise advice I would add, "and stop reading articles that tell you that not getting enough sleep can lead to Alzheimer's, ALS, and autoimmune disease," particularly if, like me, you might be a teeny bit prone to hypochondria.

A few months ago, after lying in bed like a pencil in a drawer for hours each night, trying desperately to be peaceful and instead feeling insane and judgmental ("After forty years meditating, you still can't quiet your mind?"), I decided that if I couldn't sleep, I shouldn't sleep, and that there must be something I could do that didn't require putting on lights (because as every insomniac knows, you're supposed to turn down all lights at dusk, and keep your bedroom cool and dark to facilitate ongoing melatonin release). I remembered an article in *The New Yorker* in which the author says that before the advent of electricity and artificial light, people didn't sleep through the night; they'd sleep when it got dark—Sleep One—and after a few hours, they'd wake up, congregate in small groups, and chat convivially. Then, they'd trundle off to their stacks of hay and revive themselves with more sleep, which was called Sleep Two.

Visiting friends in the middle of the night, having tea, biscuits, and a chat in flannel pajamas sounds quite civilized to me. Like these newly emergent death cafes where "strangers gather to eat cake, drink tea and discuss death . . . to help [them] make the most of their finite lives," in a sleepless cafe strangers could huddle together and discuss being awake in the middle of the night. But since I live in the forest, half an hour away from any place where insomniacs might huddle, I decided to start my own nighttime ritual.

Now when my eyes fly open at three, I follow my breath from my toes to the top of my head and back again a few times, then I do the four-seven-eight sleep breath count (four on the in breath, seven on the top of the breath, eight on the out breath). Sometimes I listen to the elegiac writing of George Eliot and if Mr. Casaubon doesn't aggravate me too much, I might fall asleep. But if I'm still awake after fifteen minutes, I say in a purposefully cheerful whisper: "Time to go visiting!" (The cheerful part is necessary to drown out and reprogram the doleful lament at not being able to sleep.) I slip into my bright pink slippers with the floppy felt turquoise flowers, pad into the dark hall with my arms outstretched like a zombie so that I don't bang into walls and trip over chairs, inch my way to the back door, exchange the slippers for my black knee-high Wellingtons (which I placed by the door the night before), put on my husband's puffy pumpkin-colored Antarctica coat, and grope for the door.

Creak, door opens.

Creak, door closes.

Step down.

Look up.

And just like that, I am in another world.

The glittering bowl of the sky is so vast that it seems as if I am upside down, like the first time I went snorkeling and saw that the ocean had an underneath: undulating anemones, knobs of rutilant coral, neon purple and green rainbow fish that must have been here all along but because I never looked below the surface, I never knew.

★   ★   ★

Outside is in, upside is down, the vastness in the sky and the space between my ribs, in my chest, and inside every cell is hollow and full, nothing and everything.

In the middle of the night, with the very first step, I feel as if I am snorkeling in the night sky, gliding around the stars, letting the consummate darkness penetrate my fevered mind. I can't believe that this "underneath" has been waiting for me all along, and if not exactly terrified of it, I've been highly suspicious of its secrets and vast mystery.

An owl hoots; the sound ricochets against the trees, between my thoughts. A mockingbird sings and the notes feel as if they are rising from my sternum. The wind chimes—the ones that, according to the salesperson from whom we bought them, have been tuned to "Amazing Grace"—rustle against each other like tiny monastery bells. As my eyes adjust to the dark I start walking, which feels like swimming.

Outside is in, upside is down, the vastness in the sky and the space between my ribs, in my chest, and inside every cell is hollow and full, nothing and everything. I open my arms as wide as I can, as if I can scoop the stars like liquid manna into my throat, chest, legs. Once, twice, three times, the arms open, scoop, take in the stars and the darkness that makes them visible while the trees, noble and immense, bear witness to this exchange of liquid light. Drenched in stillness now, my body moves back to the house, swims down the hallway, moves into bed, and dissolves like the space inside an anemone when it closes. Like the deathless beauty of no me, no you, no world.

> *You do not have to*
> *prostrate yourself at the feet of*
> *shame for one more minute or keep*
> *begging forgiveness for*
> *being yourself.*

Stop Waiting to Be Ready

Stop trying to be the self you imagine you would be if you were smarter, prettier, thinner, kinder, more accomplished than you are. You've already done that. If it didn't work the first thousand times, it's not going to work now. Or ever.

So you're still selfish.

So you're still struggling with food and your weight.

So you're still crazy in the middle of the night . . . and

sometimes in broad daylight. So is ninety-nine percent of the population.

I'm not saying to act on these feelings. I'm not advocating indulgence or collapse or despair. I'm saying it's time to stand in your own two shoes. It's time to be your own authority. You've given yourself away to programs, methods, big daddies for too long. Come back. As Glinda said to Dorothy: you've always had the power.

If you're feeling selfish, don't push it away. Don't pretend you're nicer than you feel. Turn toward the selfishness, not away from it. Let yourself feel like the most selfish person in the universe—without acting on it. Notice how it changes when you let it be there, feel it, accept it. And begin to pay attention to the noticer instead of what is noticed.

If you're eating past fullness, stop. And if you don't stop, fine—but ask yourself what's going on. Notice what you feel, what arises inside you.

Accept responsibility for your actions. You're not a child. You don't need to be regulated by an external authority, most particularly a diet.

If you don't love your work, if you feel like a failure, if you're struggling to pay your bills, if you feel unlovable or worthless or crazy in the middle of the night, take a breath. Then take another. If you have cancer, if you are dying, pay attention. Listen. Look. Breathe.

You've got a body and that body responds to what you put into it. Listen to it. If sugar makes you feel depressed, stop eating it, even if it's on your eating plan. And rather than focus on how deprived you feel, ask yourself who it is that feels deprived. She's probably five or eight or twelve. Are you?

Climb out of your mind and back into your body, even if it feels uncomfortable. Turn toward the feeling not away from it. Treat yourself the way you would treat a small child who is lost—because that part of you is.

Take yourself in. Ask the questions no one ever asked you. Keep going until you know the answer and you know who's asking. Until you realize—it's not far away—that the essence of you, like the sky, was always here. You just happened to get distracted by the local weather for a few decades.

Do whatever you have to do (you already know what it is)—move your body or unwind the trauma that's in your nervous system. Leave—or begin—that relationship. Make doing what you have to do a priority for your life, because if you don't, you leave yourself behind. And at your last breath, which will come sooner than you think, you will have missed showing up for this messy magnificent life.

You do not have to prostrate yourself at the feet of shame for one more minute or keep begging forgiveness for being yourself.

We need you.

We need you to stop waiting to be ready. To stop waiting to act until you become the self you imagine you would be if only you were different than you are.

We need your radical truth-telling, your willingness to speak from your Montana-wide heart, but most of all, we need the unrepeatable essence of you.

Come back. Now.

> *Use your eyes and see something—anything at all— as if you have just landed on planet earth.*

Touchstones for Breaking the Trance

When I finished writing *This Messy Magnificent Life*, I realized I'd been using (and teaching) a set of seven nonlinear, nonsequential touchstones that I discovered and refined during six years of writing the book. Instead of adding them to your to-do list, sigh, use them to break the trance of everyday discontent, anxiety, and lack.

If you turn any touchstone into a rule, it quickly becomes an instrument of shame and punishment.

After that—well you know what comes after that: rebellion, shame, and a series of what-the-hell's: *I knew I couldn't do this. I'm worthless. I might as well eat potato chips and drink tequila.* Be fierce about not going there.

Stand in your own two shoes.

Come out of your mind and into your body. Feel your feet on the floor, your hands at your side, your breath in your belly. Use your ears and listen to sounds. Use your eyes and see something—anything at all—as if you have just landed on planet earth. And *breathe*. If you're still powering through by gritting your teeth and holding in your stomach, take a breath. A long one. Repeat often.

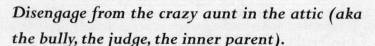

Disengage from the crazy aunt in the attic (aka the bully, the judge, the inner parent).

Everyone's got one and s/he is not your friend. She wants to keep you small by protecting you from being disloyal to what once brought you love. Until you understand that she is wrong and that she is not you, true change is not possible.

Be kind to the ghost children.

Ghost children are parts of yourself based on memories, earlier impressions, and associations. They are frozen in time and see all of the present through memories of past painful experiences. Shower them with curiosity and tenderness. Watch them melt.

Stop believing your thoughts.

You are not your beliefs, opinions, emotions, or thoughts. Know the difference between what happens and your thoughts and interpretations of what happens. Between an actual experience and your reaction to it. Most of our thoughts, beliefs, and opinions are rigid, reactive, and wildly out of touch with our present situation. They can also lead to unnecessary anxiety, stress, and perceiving others as enemies that need to be vanquished.

Drop the war.

End the Me Project. Stop trying to get rid of, improve, resist, or otherwise fix yourself. With kindness, turn toward—not away from—what you believe you have to get rid of. In that turn, you will discover that demons become angels and the scary snakes of your life become harmless strands of rope.

Ask yourself "What's not wrong?"

Do this five times a day for ten seconds at a time. You will be stunned at what happens when you see that it's almost always your mind, not the situation, that makes you miserable.

Pay attention to what remains.

When you are not possessed by your thoughts and stop taking yourself to be what happens to you, the background becomes foreground, what was up is down, and the noticer rather than the noticed is revealed. It's better than chocolate. Better than sex. Better than the perfect pair of boots. It's what you wanted from getting those things, multiplied by a quadrillion.

In Grateful Acknowledgment

I can't imagine this book (or my life) without the people whom it is my kiss-the-ground good fortune to know:

Peter Guzzardi for editorial class and grace beyond measure; Celeste Fine for being and giving what I didn't realize I needed; Anne Lamott for friendship, words, and unremitting generosity; Scott Edelstein for brilliance in the eleventh hour; Stewart Emery for being craft's (and my) fervent champion; Sarah Passick for chutzpah; Barbara Graham for consistent and oh so wise counsel; Susan Moldow, Nan Graham, and Roz Lippel for seeing the vision and insisting on it; Catherine Ingram for meeting me in the time-space warp; Barbara Renshaw for twelve life-changing years; Jeanne Rosenblum for pink love enduring; Kim Rosen for lushness and language and insight; Jace Schinderman for a lifetime of staying the course; Lauren Matthews for rapture and magnificence; Joan Emery, Alice Josephs, and Stephen

Josephs for caring so deeply so many times; Kirtana for morning song; Allison Post for sweetheart healing; Sally-anne McCartin for perspective, kindness, and wicked humor; Katie Monaghan and the Scribner team for their unflagging support; Sufi for enduring guidance; John Mini for Taoist magic; Luanne Lansing for lavishing support; Robert Werner for body fluency; Claire Zammit, Katie Hendricks, and Arielle Ford for cheerleading of the spirit; my retreat students for their bright flames; Judy Ross for being so good at so much; Jane Armytage, Menno de Lange, and Doriena Wolff for being the team of dreams; Richard Wiggs for a lifetime of steadfast kindness; Ruth Wiggs for sass, style, and clear seeing; Howard Roth, for his ever-generous Snoball heart and humor in spite of it all. And Matt Weinstein for being the light inside the dark. Of everything.

About the Author

Geneen Roth is the author of ten books, including the *New York Times* bestsellers *When Food Is Love*, *Lost and Found*, and *Women Food and God*, as well as *The Craggy Hole in My Heart and the Cat Who Fixed It*. She has been speaking, teaching groundbreaking workshops, and offering retreats for over thirty years and has appeared on numerous national shows, including *The Oprah Winfrey Show*, *20/20*, the *Today* show, *Good Morning America*, and *The View*. For more information about her work, please visit GeneenRoth.com.